The Easier You Make It, The Better It Tastes

Jayni and Frank Carey

BETTER HOMES AND GARDENS® BOOKS
Des Moines, Iowa

BETTER HOMES AND GARDENS® BOOKS
An Imprint of Meredith® Books
President, Book Group: Joseph J. Ward
Vice President and Editorial Director: Elizabeth P. Rice
Executive Editor: Nancy N. Green
Managing Editor: Christopher Cavanaugh
Art Director: Ernest Shelton
Test Kitchen Director: Sharon Stilwell

The Easier You Make It, The Better It Tastes
Authors: Jayni and Frank Carey
Editor: Jennifer Darling
Graphic Designer: Lynda Haupert
Test Kitchen Product Supervisor: Marilyn Cornelius
Food Stylists: Lynn Blanchard, Janet Pittman
Food Photographer: Andy Lyons
Portrait Photographer: H. Jay Carey
Copy Editor: Jennifer Speer Ramundt

On the cover: Smoked Chicken on Pasta with Tomatoes (page 78)

Meredith Corporation Corporate Officers:
Chairman of the Executive Committee: E. T. Meredith III
Chairman of the Board, President, and Chief Executive Officer: Jack D. Rehm
Group Presidents: Joseph J. Ward, Books; William T. Kerr, Magazines; Philip A. Jones, Broadcasting; Allen L. Sabbag, Real Estate
Vice Presidents: Leo R. Armatis, Corporate Relations; Thomas G. Fisher, General Counsel and Secretary; Larry D. Hartsook, Finance; Michael A. Sell, Treasurer; Kathleen J. Zehr, Controller and Assistant Secretary

Preface

It isn't often that we lend the Better Homes and Gardens® name to a cookbook written by people outside our family of Better Homes and Gardens® Cookbook Editors. But then, it isn't often that we find a couple like Frank and Jayni Carey, whose cooking sensibilities so nearly match our own.

Like most book publishers, we receive thousands of manuscript submissions each year. Somehow, the Careys' submission stood out from the very beginning. Their philosophy of cooking—their search for the pleasure and adventure in what is too often perceived to be a chore—and their manner of presenting information to the reader fit so well with our own that we simply had to take their recipes to our kitchens.

The Test Kitchen's experience confirmed our instincts. Every recipe in this book was tested thoroughly, and met all of our Test Kitchen's rigorous standards. The Carey's recipes proved to be unique, irresistible—*and* our testing procedures assure that they'll work for you.

Finally, in meetings of small groups, we asked our readers what they thought of a cookbook that made gourmet-style cooking simple. Our readers gave the Careys' idea the final seal of approval—telling us this was, in fact, something they wanted.

Today, we're not only happy to have teamed up with Frank and Jayni, we're thrilled to be delivering copies of THE EASIER YOU MAKE IT, THE BETTER IT TASTES so that you, too, can finally experience firsthand the joys of gourmet-quality meals without the gourmet fuss.

Introduction

The title, *The Easier You Make It, The Better It Tastes*, rings true. We look forward to preparing meals and consider it a pleasurable experience. Like most working couples, we want to prepare meals that are satisfying and elegant, but our time is limited. Together, we've created recipes that are easy to prepare, yet fulfill our desire for interesting meals. Our recipes cut preparation time, but still let every meal we put on the table be one we can be proud of. What could be easier than fresh sea scallops grilled over an apple wood charcoal fire and sauced with an easy-to-make mustard-marmalade? Chicken slowly simmered in Port wine with herbs and shallots can be just as simple and equally delicious. And consider savory lamb chops, quickly sautéed and topped with a light wine and herb sauce, made right in the pan. These are just a few examples of our elegant, but easy, style.

Our Midwestern upbringing has taught us that recipes need not be complicated to be delicious, nor extravagant to be appreciated. We sometimes relish the challenge of preparing complex meals and have labored to replicate exotic dishes for friends and family. But surprisingly, it has been the simple meals that have left a lasting impression. Simple, not only because the steps to create them are few, but also because their flavors are clear, honest, and fresh.

Our recipes are designed for people who expect impressive results without a lot of time and fuss. Cooking doesn't have to be complicated, time-consuming, or mysterious. Preparing simple, elegant meals requires no extraordinary talent, just three essential ingredients: imaginative recipes, high-quality ingredients, and—most important—clear, complete instructions in an easy-to-use format. Most everyone wants to successfully master a few favorite dishes, and our simple approach to cooking will encourage even reluctant cooks to try their hands in the kitchen.

In this book, you'll find a large selection of recipes for nearly every occasion. When entertaining, you can choose from casual entrées cooked on the grill to sophisticated dishes fit for candlelight and romance. We offer recipes seasoned from regional America and exotic dishes spiced with world flavors. When cooking for the family, you'll find nutritional, easy-to-fix meals everyone will like. Our approach to "small batch" preserving brings the freshness of summer to the table long after the garden is gone. And to complement today's quick, easy meals, we offer satisfying, but simple, desserts.

We enjoy cooking together and sharing our culinary adventures. The time we spend in the kitchen soothes the stresses of our busy lifestyles. We discovered along the way that what we once thought of as sharing the work, now means sharing the fun. The key is delicious, easy-to-prepare meals. We hope our recipes will help others find, as we have found, the rewards that come from sharing in the creation of a meal.

Jayni and Frank Carey

Contents

Quick Starts.............

A special appetizer can set your meal apart. Try one of our tasty recipes or adapt our easy Party Favors to your specific entertaining needs.

Tuscan Bean Dip

This delicately flavored dip made with cannellini beans can serve as a party appetizer or a starter for an Italian meal. Serve with crisp bread sticks. Instead of soaking the beans overnight, you can cover them with water, bring the water to a boil, and simmer for 2 minutes. Remove the pan from the heat and let the beans stand, covered, for 1 hour. Drain and continue as directed.

½ cup dry cannellini beans
1 teaspoon olive oil
3 cloves garlic, peeled
2 fresh sage leaves
1 sprig Italian parsley
1 sprig thyme

●●●

2 tablespoons extra virgin olive oil
½ teaspoon salt
⅛ teaspoon white pepper
Lemon juice

●●●

Sage leaves
Extra virgin olive oil
Bread sticks

Rinse the beans, and soak them overnight in cold water. Drain the beans, and place them in a medium-size pan or Dutch oven. Add enough cold water to cover the beans by about 2 inches. Add 1 teaspoon of olive oil and the garlic. Make a bouquet of the sage, Italian parsley, and thyme, and tie the stems together with string. Place the herb bouquet in the pan of beans, and bring the water to a boil. Reduce the heat to low; cover and simmer the beans for 1 to 1½ hours. Uncover after 45 minutes, check the beans, and add more water, if necessary. Continue cooking, adding water when needed, until the beans are very soft and most of the water has evaporated. Remove from the heat, and cool for 10 minutes.

Remove the herb bouquet, and pour the beans and garlic cloves into a food processor fitted with a steel blade. Add the 2 tablespoons extra virgin olive oil, salt, and white pepper, and puree until the beans are smooth. Pour the bean puree into a serving bowl, and stir in lemon juice to taste. Garnish with sage leaves and drizzle with extra virgin olive oil. Serve with bread sticks.

Serves 8 to 10

Per serving: 74 calories, 2 g protein, 7 g carbohydrate, 4 g total fat (1 g saturated), 0 mg cholesterol, 135 mg sodium, 196 mg potassium

Marinated Yogurt Cheese

Marinated in olive oil with sliced olives and herbs, this soft cheese is delicious served with crusty French bread. The cheese may also be tossed with hot pasta or used as a filling in twice-baked potatoes.

2 16-ounce cartons plain low-fat yogurt
   (no gelatin added)
½ teaspoon salt

Marinade:

1½ cups extra virgin olive oil
 3 cloves garlic, minced
 1 teaspoon herbes de Provence, crushed
⅔ cup green olives, sliced

●●●

French bread or crackers

Place the yogurt in a bowl, and stir in the salt. Place a large wire-mesh strainer over a large bowl. Line the strainer with several layers of cheesecloth. Spoon the yogurt into the cheesecloth. Place in the refrigerator for 12 hours to drain liquids from the yogurt. Then, carefully turn the yogurt over onto a new piece of cheesecloth (it will be somewhat firm); place in strainer and refrigerate at least 12 hours more.

Marinade: Combine the olive oil, garlic, and herbes de Provence in a saucepan, and heat over low heat for 3 to 4 minutes or just until the mixture is very warm. Remove from heat, and cool to room temperature. Add the sliced olives.

Scoop spoonfuls of the yogurt cheese into a container. Pour the marinade over the cheese. Cover container tightly with a lid. Refrigerate at least 24 hours before using. (Store up to 1 week in the refrigerator.)

When ready to serve, let yogurt set in its container at room temperature for about 30 minutes to liquify the oil. Spoon large dollops of the yogurt cheese into the center of a shallow bowl. Spoon some of the marinade around the cheese. Serve with French bread or crackers.

Makes about forty 1-tablespoon servings

Per serving: 44 calories, 1 g protein, 1 g carbohydrate, 4 g total fat (1 g saturated), 1 mg cholesterol, 60 mg sodium, 27 mg potassium

Cross-Culture Mushrooms

Most supermarkets and specialty food stores have a large variety of fresh mushrooms available. Choose several different kinds for outstanding flavor and an interesting presentation. Try them on a grilled steak sandwich!

8 ounces assorted fresh mushrooms, rinsed (button, morel, oyster, crimini, shiitake)

8 cloves garlic, peeled and cut in half

•••

1 tablespoon lemon juice

1 tablespoon snipped fresh parsley

1½ teaspoons snipped fresh marjoram or ¼ teaspoon dried marjoram, crushed

1½ teaspoons snipped fresh thyme or ¼ teaspoon dried thyme, crushed

1½ teaspoons snipped fresh tarragon or ¼ teaspoon dried tarragon, crushed

⅛ teaspoon salt

6 tablespoons olive oil

•••

¾ cup apple wood smoking chips

Prepare the mushrooms and garlic as directed. Halve or quarter large mushrooms. Place mushrooms and garlic in a large bowl.

In a small bowl, combine the lemon juice, parsley, marjoram, thyme, tarragon, parsley, and salt. Slowly whisk in the olive oil. Pour the mixture over the mushrooms and garlic, and gently toss to combine.

Place the mushrooms on a large piece of aluminum foil. Close the foil over the mushrooms, leaving the top open slightly.

Place the smoking chips on another piece of aluminum foil. Seal tightly to make a foil packet. Poke a few holes in the foil to allow the smoke to escape.

To grill over indirect heat, divide the hot coals, banking them on the sides of the grill and leaving an empty space in the center. Place the foil packet of smoking chips directly on some of the hot coals. Place the foil containing the mushrooms and garlic on the grill rack directly over the empty space surrounded by the coals. Cover the grill, and cook for 30 to 45 minutes or until the mushrooms are tender and the garlic is soft.

Serves 4

Per serving: 212 calories, 1 g protein, 8 g carbohydrate, 20 g total fat (3 g saturated), 0 mg cholesterol, 71 mg sodium, 176 mg potassium

Smoked Crimini Mushrooms

In this recipe, Italian mushrooms and a roasted red pepper are tossed with lemon juice, garlic, herbs, and olive oil, then smoked over hot coals. Serve this savory dish as an appetizer or as a side dish for grilled beef or lamb.

1 red sweet pepper
8 ounces fresh crimini mushrooms, rinsed

•••

1 tablespoon lemon juice
3 garlic cloves, minced
1 tablespoon fresh Italian parsley, finely chopped
½ teaspoon dried oregano
⅛ teaspoon salt
⅓ cup olive oil

•••

¾ cup apple wood, cherry wood, or mesquite smoking chips

Slice the sweet red pepper in half lengthwise, and remove the stem, seeds, and pith. Lay the pepper pieces, cut sides down, on a cookie sheet, and place under the oven broiler. Broil for about 5 minutes or until the skin begins to wrinkle and char. Remove the pepper pieces from the oven, and immediately enclose them in a paper bag for about 20 minutes to steam for easier peeling. Peel the pepper pieces, and slice them into ½-inch strips.

Rinse the mushrooms. Place mushrooms and roasted pepper strips in a large bowl.

In a small bowl, combine the lemon juice, garlic, parsley, oregano, and salt. Slowly whisk in the olive oil. Pour the mixture over the mushrooms and pepper strips, and gently toss to combine. Place the mushrooms and pepper strips on a large piece of aluminum foil. Close the foil over the mushrooms and pepper strips, leaving the top open slightly.

Place the smoking chips on another piece of aluminum foil. Seal tightly to make a foil packet. Poke a few holes in the foil to allow the smoke to escape.

To grill over indirect heat, divide the hot coals, banking them on the sides of the grill and leaving an empty space in the center. Place the foil packet of smoking chips directly on some of the hot coals. Place the foil containing the mushrooms and peppers on the grill rack directly over the empty space surrounded by the coals. Cover the grill, and cook for 30 to 45 minutes or until the mushrooms are tender.

Serves 4

Per serving: 182 calories, 2 g protein, 5 g carbohydrate, 18 g total fat (2 g saturated), 0 mg cholesterol, 70 mg sodium, 262 mg potassium

Spicy Louisiana Shrimp

Serve spicy, Cajun-style shrimp as a starter course to Bayou Chicken (page 57) or Ragin' Cajun Rib Eyes (page 91).

24 medium-size fresh shrimp

Seasoning Mix:
  4 teaspoons paprika
  2 teaspoons onion powder
  2 teaspoons garlic powder
  1 teaspoon black pepper
  ½ teaspoon cayenne pepper
  1 teaspoon dried thyme, crushed
  1 teaspoon dried oregano, crushed

  •••

  2 tablespoons butter
  2 tablespoons olive oil

  •••

4 lemon wedges

Shell and devein the shrimp, leaving the tails on.

Seasoning Mix: In a shallow bowl, combine paprika, onion powder, garlic powder, black pepper, cayenne pepper, thyme, and oregano. Dust the shrimp with the seasoning mix and set aside.

In a large skillet, heat the butter and olive oil over medium heat. Add all of the shrimp at once. Sauté for 1 to 2 minutes per side or till shrimp turn pink. Serve with lemon wedges.

Serves 4

Per serving: 175 calories, 8 g protein, 4 g carbohydrate, 14 g total fat (5 g saturated), 70 mg cholesterol, 210 mg sodium, 164 mg potassium

Party Favors

Let these easy party foods provide an elegant touch to the next event you host. We provide the ideas and suggestions; you tailor the amounts and ingredients to suit your special occasion.

Smoked Oyster Dip

Soften an 8-ounce package of cream cheese. Drain a 3¼-ounce can of smoked oysters, and pour the oysters over the cream cheese. Top with bottled cocktail sauce. Serve with assorted crackers.

Fruits of the Sea

Arrange an assortment of shellfish on a large serving dish. We suggest hot or cold spiced shrimp, oysters on the half shell, crab claws, steamed clams, and mussels. Serve with warm melted butter, lemon wedges, and your favorite seafood cocktail sauce. Have seafood forks or toothpicks available.

Chutney Cheese Ball

Soften two 8-ounce packages of cream cheese. Blend in ½ cup mango chutney along with 2 teaspoons curry powder and ½ teaspoon dry mustard. Chill mixture for several hours. Roll into a ball, cover with ½ cup coarsely chopped toasted almonds, and serve with extra chutney.

Artichokes

Trim fresh artichokes, and boil them in water with 1 tablespoon of lemon juice or vinegar until tender. Serve with melted butter and lemon wedges or a mixture of ¼ cup mayonnaise and ½ to 1 teaspoon horseradish.

Marinated Artichokes

Drain canned artichoke hearts, and slice them in half. Marinate in your favorite bottled Italian vinaigrette for at least 1 hour before serving.

Vegetable Plate

Slice an assortment of crunchy vegetables, and arrange them on a serving tray. We suggest carrots, celery, radishes, broccoli, cauliflower, cucumbers, green onions, cherry tomatoes, and green, red, and yellow sweet peppers. Serve with sour cream flavored to taste with your favorite herbs. Add lemon juice, black pepper, green peppercorns, minced onion, or garlic for extra flavor.

Mexican Dip and Chips

Shape a can of refried beans into a mound on a serving dish. Spread a layer of guacamole on the beans. Add a layer of sour cream, and top with shredded cheddar cheese. Garnish with chopped green onion, black olives, and cherry tomatoes. Serve with tortilla chips and a bowl of chunky salsa.

Tortilla Pinwheels

Mix 8 ounces sour cream with 8 ounces softened cream cheese. Add ¼ cup finely chopped green onions, 1 minced garlic clove, a dash of cayenne pepper, and lime juice to taste. Spread mixture on flour tortillas (about ¼ cup per 5-inch tortilla); place a layer of spinach or lettuce leaves over cream cheese mixture. Roll up tightly, and chill 1 to 6 hours. When ready to serve, slice tortillas into 1-inch pieces. Arrange on a serving tray and serve with salsa for dipping.

Toasted Garlic Rounds

Cut a loaf of French bread into ¾-inch slices. Spread slices in a single layer on a baking sheet. Bake at 325° for 12 minutes. Remove bread from oven. With a pastry brush, lightly brush both sides of each slice with olive oil. Turn slices over, and return bread to oven. Bake about 12 minutes more or until bread is completely dry and golden brown. Rub each piece with a cut garlic clove. Serve with liver pâté or an assortment of meats and cheeses.

Fruit Plate

Arrange fresh fruit on an attractive plate. We suggest melon balls, kiwi slices, pineapple rings, sliced mangos, strawberries, cherries, grapes, and berries. For dipping, serve fruit with bowls of plain yogurt, granola, and sweetened whipped cream flavored with orange liqueur.

Strawberries 'n' Cream

Whip softened cream cheese with a spoonful of powdered sugar; add additional powdered sugar to reach desired sweetness. Add a dash of cinnamon. Thin mixture with a small amount of half-and-half, light cream, or milk until a dipping consistency is reached. Pour mixture into a small bowl, and surround bowl with large, juicy strawberries for dipping.

Chocolate Fondue

Heat hot fudge sauce in a fondue pot. For extra flavor add chocolate, coffee, orange, or almond liqueur. For dipping we suggest pound cake, butter cookies, pretzels, pineapple chunks, apple slices, cherries, bananas, strawberries, or anything that goes well with chocolate; this is an opportunity for you to be creative.

Prime Cuts

Hearty main dishes featuring beef, pork, veal, and even lamb chops await you. It's your chance to make something new for dinner tonight!

Beef Tenderloin Filets with Mushrooms

After cooking the filets, combine the pan drippings with green onions, mushrooms, red wine, and brandy for a robust sauce that can be made in minutes.

2 teaspoons cracked pepper
4 beef tenderloin filets, cut 1 to
    1½ inches thick
1 tablespoon butter or margarine
1 tablespoon olive oil
   Salt

•••

4 green onions, chopped
2 cups sliced fresh mushrooms

•••

½ cup dry red wine
¼ cup brandy

Rub ½ teaspoon of the pepper onto each filet. In a large skillet, heat the butter or margarine and olive oil over medium-high heat. Add the filets; cook for 3 to 5 minutes or until browned. Turn the meat over and sprinkle with salt. Continue cooking for 3 to 5 minutes more or until meat is of desired doneness. Remove filets from skillet and keep warm.

Add the green onions and mushrooms to the skillet. Cook and stir over medium heat until the green onions are soft and the mushrooms are brown (2 to 3 minutes).

Carefully add the wine and brandy. Bring to a boil over medium-high heat, stirring occasionally. Cook until sauce is reduced by about half. Pour sauce over filets and serve immediately.

Serves 4

Per serving: 391 calories, 37 g protein, 3 g carbohydrate, 19 g total fat (7 g saturated), 115 mg cholesterol, 146 mg sodium, 729 mg potassium

Steaks with Red Wine Sauce

Even those who grill their steaks will appreciate this sautéed version. After cooking the steaks, make a sauce of shallots, red wine, and brandy. Parsnips cooked until very tender, then mashed, make a tasty accompaniment to this robust sauce.

4 beef top loin steaks, cut 1 inch thick (about 3½ pounds)
1 tablespoon olive oil
Salt

•••

¼ cup chopped shallots
1 tablespoon butter or margarine

•••

½ cup dry red wine
¼ cup brandy
¼ teaspoon instant beef bouillon granules
Dash pepper

Brush steaks lightly with olive oil.

Preheat a wide, heavy skillet over high heat till very hot. Add steaks. Reduce heat to medium. Cook, uncovered, for 3 to 6 minutes or until browned. Turn the steaks over and sprinkle with salt. Cook for 3 to 6 minutes more or until meat is of desired doneness. Remove steaks from skillet; keep warm.

Add the shallots and butter or margarine to the skillet. Cook and stir until soft. Add the red wine, brandy, beef bouillon, and pepper. Increase heat to medium-high, and bring the sauce to a boil. Cook, stirring frequently, until the sauce is reduced by half. Pour sauce over the steaks and serve immediately.

Serves 4

Per serving: 463 calories, 49 g protein, 3 g carbohydrate, 22 g total fat (8 g saturated), 138 mg cholesterol, 237 mg sodium, 754 mg potassium

Hot Beef Curry

When cold weather settles in, instead of the usual chili or stew, warm up your family with this spicy beef dish. Hot curry powder can be found at specialty stores selling Indian spices.

2 tablespoons olive oil
2 cups coarsely chopped onion
1 green sweet pepper, chopped (¾ cup)

•••

2 pounds boneless top round steak, trimmed and cut into 1½-inch-long strips
2 14½-ounce cans tomatoes, cut up
2 tablespoons curry powder
½ teaspoon salt

•••

Hot cooked basmati rice or long grain rice

Heat the olive oil in a large skillet or Dutch oven over medium-high heat. Add the onion and green pepper; cook and stir until vegetables are tender. Remove the vegetables from the skillet.

Add ⅓ of the meat to the skillet. Cook and stir until browned; remove from skillet. Repeat with remaining meat. Return all of the meat and the vegetables to the skillet. Stir in the undrained tomatoes, curry powder, and salt. Bring the mixture to a boil, cover, and reduce the heat to low. Simmer about 1 hour or until the meat is tender. Serve immediately over rice.

Serves 6

Per serving: 412 calories, 35 g protein, 41 g carbohydrate, 11 g total fat (3 g saturated), 72 mg cholesterol, 469 mg sodium, 887 mg potassium

Caraway Pork Roast with Madeira Sauce

A side dish of tender butternut or acorn squash wedges complement the rich, savory, brown sauce.

2 pounds boneless pork loin or sirloin
    roast
2 teaspoons caraway seed, slightly
    crushed
¼ teaspoon salt
¼ teaspoon pepper

       ●●●

2 tablespoons olive oil
½ cup chopped carrot
½ cup chopped celery
⅓ cup chopped onion
2 large cloves garlic, peeled
2 tablespoons dry Madeira

Madeira Sauce:

1 cup beef broth
¼ cup dry Madeira
¼ cup cold water
1 tablespoon cornstarch

Trim excess fat from the roast. Rub caraway seed over the entire piece of meat. Sprinkle with salt and pepper.

Heat the olive oil in a large ovenproof skillet over medium-high heat. Add the pork roast, carrot, celery, onion, and garlic to the skillet. Brown the roast on all sides. Pour 2 tablespoons Madeira over the roast and vegetables. Bake the roast, uncovered, in a 325° oven for 1 to 1¼ hours or until the internal temperature reaches 160°. Remove the roast, leaving the vegetables in the skillet. Cover the roast to keep warm.

Madeira Sauce: Carefully add the beef broth and ¼ cup Madeira to the skillet. Bring the mixture to a boil over medium-high heat. Boil about 5 minutes or until the sauce is reduced by about ⅓. Strain the broth (you should have about ½ cup), and discard the vegetables. Skim excess fat from the broth. Return the broth to the skillet. Combine the cornstarch and water; add the mixture to the broth. Cook and stir till thickened and bubbly. Cook and stir for 1 minute more. Carve the roast into thick slices. To serve, spoon sauce over meat.

Serves 6

Per serving: 345 calories, 31 g protein, 5 g carbohydrate, 21 g total fat (6 g saturated), 103 mg cholesterol, 317 mg sodium, 541 mg potassium

Pork with Apples and Cream

A sauce of poached apples and cream makes a rich topping for sautéed pork loin.

1 pound pork loin, sliced ½ inch thick
   or one 1-pound pork tenderloin
¼ teaspoon salt
⅛ teaspoon pepper
¼ cup all-purpose flour
   •••
3 tablespoons butter or margarine
½ cup cider vinegar
¼ cup sugar
¼ cup Applejack or apple juice
1 large apple (Granny Smith preferred),
   cored and sliced
   •••
⅔ cup whipping cream

If using the pork tenderloin, cut it into 4 equal portions. With the flat side of a meat mallet, pound each piece between 2 sheets of waxed paper or plastic wrap to ¼-inch thickness.

Sprinkle both sides of the pork loin or pounded tenderloin pieces with salt and pepper, then coat with flour.

In a 12-inch skillet over medium-high heat, brown the meat quickly in the butter or margarine for 3 to 5 minutes or until no pink remains.

Remove the meat from the skillet. Add the vinegar, sugar, and Applejack to the skillet. Reduce the heat to medium. Stir to dissolve the sugar; add apple slices. Let the apple slices poach in the liquid until they are cooked and the sauce reduces and becomes syrupy (about 8 minutes).

Stir in the whipping cream. Return the meat to the skillet; heat through, spooning the sauce over the meat. Transfer the meat to a serving platter. Arrange the apple slices over the meat, and spoon the sauce on top.

Serves 4

Per serving: 500 calories, 26 g protein, 29 g carbohydrate, 28 g total fat (16 g saturated), 157 mg cholesterol, 294 mg sodium, 590 mg potassium

Pork Chops with Vermouth

The economical pork chop has been neglected for far too long. By creating a simple sauce of vermouth and herbs, you'll discover the elegance hidden in an old favorite.

4 pork loin chops, cut ½ inch thick
   (about 1¼ pounds)
  Salt
  Pepper
1 tablespoon butter or margarine
1 tablespoon olive oil

• • •

⅓ cup dry vermouth
⅛ teaspoon dried marjoram, crushed, or
   ½ teaspoon fresh snipped marjoram
⅛ teaspoon dried thyme, crushed, or
   ½ teaspoon fresh snipped thyme

Sprinkle the pork chops with salt and pepper. In a large skillet, heat the butter and olive oil over medium heat. Add the pork chops and cook for 3 to 5 minutes on each side or until no pink remains and juices run clear.

Remove the pork chops from skillet; keep warm. Add the vermouth, marjoram, and thyme to the skillet. Increase the heat to medium-high; simmer, stirring constantly, for 2 to 3 minutes or until liquid reduces and thickens slightly.

Pour the sauce over pork chops and serve immediately.

Serves 4

Per serving: 229 calories, 18 g protein, 1 g carbohydrate, 14 g total fat (5 g saturated), 66 mg cholesterol, 106 mg sodium, 240 mg potassium

Poor Richard's Pork Chops

Indoors or out, this simple yet tasty meat goes well with steamed vegetables or a mixed green salad.

4 pork chops, cut ¾ inch thick
  (about 1½ to 2 pounds)
  Salt
  Pepper
4 teaspoons coarse brown mustard

Sprinkle each pork chop with salt and pepper. Spread ½ teaspoon of the mustard on each side of each pork chop. Place the pork chops on the unheated rack of a broiler pan. Broil 6 inches from the heat for 7 to 10 minutes on each side or until no pink remains and juices run clear.

Or, to grill, place the chops on a an uncovered grill directly over medium-hot coals. Grill for 8 to 11 minutes, turning once, or until no pink remains and juices run clear.

Serves 4

Per serving: 230 calories, 27 g protein, 1 g carbohydrate, 12 g total fat (4 g saturated), 87 mg cholesterol, 159 mg sodium, 352 mg potassium

Veal with Lemon Dijon Cream

Impressive yet simple, this veal entrée can be made in minutes. If your grocer doesn't have veal scallops, use 1 pound of boneless veal leg top round steak cut into four pieces. With the flat side of a meat mallet, pound each piece between two sheets of waxed paper or plastic wrap to ⅛-inch thickness.

4 to 8 veal scallops (¾ to 1 pound)
Pepper

•••

2 tablespoons butter or margarine
2 cups fresh sliced mushrooms
1 tablespoon lemon juice

•••

2 tablespoons butter or margarine
¼ cup brandy

•••

½ cup whipping cream
1 teaspoon Dijon-style mustard

Sprinkle meat lightly with pepper.

Melt 2 tablespoons of butter or margarine in a large skillet. Sauté sliced mushrooms over medium-high heat for 2 to 3 minutes. Add the lemon juice, and cook until the liquid is evaporated (1 to 3 minutes). Remove the mushrooms from skillet.

Add the remaining 2 tablespoons of butter or margarine to skillet. Cook the veal scallops, half at a time, over medium-high heat for 1 to 2 minutes on each side. Add more butter or margarine, if necessary.

Remove the pan from heat source, add the brandy, and set aflame. Shake lightly until the flame dies. Remove the veal from the pan and keep warm.

Return the mushrooms to pan, and add whipping cream and mustard. Stir over medium-high heat until sauce bubbles and thickens slightly. Pour sauce over veal and serve immediately.

Serves 4

Per serving: 345 calories, 21 g protein, 4 g carbohydrate, 25 g total fat (10 g saturated), 107 mg cholesterol, 192 mg sodium, 417 mg potassium

Lasagne Mexicana

Layer this Mexican dish as you would lasagne, using flour tortillas instead of noodles. Serve with crunchy tortilla chips and a spicy salsa.

¾ **pound ground beef**
½ **cup chopped onion**
1 **15½-ounce can red beans, drained and rinsed**
1 **4-ounce can chopped green chilies**
1 **tablespoon chili powder**
½ **teaspoon salt**
¼ **teaspoon pepper**

•••

1 **16-ounce bottle salsa or 2 cups Tomato Salsa (page 196)**
3 **9-inch flour tortillas**
1 **8-ounce carton dairy sour cream**
2 **cups shredded Monterey jack cheese (8 ounces)**
1 **2¼-ounce can sliced pitted ripe olives, drained**

•••

3 **cups shredded lettuce**

In a large saucepan or Dutch oven, brown the ground beef with the onion over medium heat. Drain off excess fat. Add the beans, green chilies, chili powder, salt, and pepper to the saucepan. Simmer, uncovered, over low heat for 5 minutes to blend flavors, stirring occasionally.

To assemble, place ¼ cup of the salsa in the bottom of a 2-quart square baking dish. Place a tortilla in dish. Spread with ⅓ of the sour cream, ⅓ of the ground beef mixture, ⅓ of the remaining salsa, and top with ⅓ of the cheese. Repeat layers twice.

Bake, uncovered, in a 350° oven about 25 to 30 minutes or until the cheese has melted and the casserole is bubbly. Remove from oven and top with olives. Let stand for 10 minutes. Serve with shredded lettuce.

Serves 6

Per serving: 511 calories, 29 g protein, 34 g carbohydrate, 29 g total fat (15 g saturated), 93 mg cholesterol, 1,582 mg sodium, 725 mg potassium

Bistro Lamb Chops

Sautéed lamb chops are de rigeur on Parisian bistro menus. As individual as the chefs themselves, variations often follow regional flavors. Here, with garlic, tomato, wine, and herbes de Provence, it is a dish of the South. For convenience and less waste, use tomato paste sold in a tube.

8 rib or 4 loin lamb chops, cut ¾ inch
    thick (about 2 pounds)
  Pepper
2 tablespoons olive oil
  Salt

          •••

1 teaspoon tomato paste
2 cloves garlic, minced
¼ cup dry white wine or chicken broth
¼ cup chicken broth
½ teaspoon herbes de Provence, crushed

Trim the fat from the lamb chops; sprinkle with pepper. Heat the olive oil in a large skillet over medium-high heat. Add the lamb chops and cook about 3 minutes or until brown. Turn over and sprinkle with salt. Cook for 2 minutes more. Cover the skillet; reduce heat to low. Cook the lamb chops for 3 to 5 minutes more or until desired doneness.

Remove the lamb chops from the skillet and keep warm. Stir the tomato paste and garlic into the drippings in the skillet. Carefully add the wine, chicken broth, and herbes de Provence. Increase heat to medium-high; simmer about 3 minutes or until the sauce is reduced by about half, stirring frequently. Spoon off fat.

Pour the sauce over the lamb chops and serve immediately.

Serves 4

Per serving: 272 calories, 28 g protein, 1 g carbohydrate, 16 g total fat (4 g saturated), 87 mg cholesterol, 181 mg sodium, 382 mg potassium

Chicken Supreme

From elegant to everyday, chicken main dishes soar in this chapter. Take a good look; you won't believe the number of ways chicken can be prepared.

Artichoke Chicken

Hot cooked rice or noodles are a nice accompaniment to this saucy dish.

6 medium skinless, boneless chicken
    breast halves (1½ pounds)
    Salt (optional)

Topping:

¼ cup butter or margarine
1 tablespoon lemon juice
2 cloves garlic, minced
1 teaspoon dried basil or 1 tablespoon
    snipped fresh basil
1 13-ounce can artichoke hearts,
    drained and coarsely chopped
1 cup fresh white bread crumbs
    (about 1½ slices)
½ cup grated Romano cheese

••••

½ cup chicken broth
½ cup dry white wine

Rinse the chicken; pat dry with paper towels. Place the chicken breasts in a 3-quart rectangular baking dish. Sprinkle with salt, if desired, and set aside.

Topping: Melt the butter or margarine in a saucepan. Add the lemon juice, garlic, and basil. Stir in the artichokes. Add the bread crumbs and Romano cheese, and toss lightly.

Cover the chicken with the topping. Combine the chicken broth and white wine, and pour over the chicken. Bake, uncovered, in a 400° oven for 30 minutes or until the chicken is tender and no longer pink and the topping is lightly browned.

Serves 6

Per serving: 311 calories, 32 g protein, 10 g carbohydrate, 14 g total fat (7 g saturated), 102 mg cholesterol, 374 mg sodium, 421 mg potassium

Chicken with Leek and White Wine

Chicken and leeks are a stylish combination. A light wine sauce made from the pan juices finishes this simple dish. To select the freshest leeks, look for good color, crisp leaves, and no blemishes.

4 medium skinless, boneless chicken
    breast halves (1 pound)
½ cup all-purpose flour
½ teaspoon salt
1 teaspoon freshly ground pepper

•••

1 large leek
¼ cup butter or margarine

•••

½ cup dry white wine or dry vermouth

Rinse the chicken and pat dry with paper towels; set aside. In a medium bowl, combine the flour, salt, and pepper. Coat the chicken breasts with the flour mixture. Pound them gently between 2 sheets of waxed paper or plastic wrap to a uniform thickness of ⅜ inch. Use additional flour, as necessary, to keep chicken from sticking to the waxed paper. Set aside.

Peel away any dry outer leaves of the leek. Cut off the green tops about 1 inch above the white section, and remove the roots. To remove any sand, slice the leek in half lengthwise and rinse each half thoroughly under cold running water. Shake off excess water, and slice the leek into half rounds ⅛-inch thick.

Melt the butter or margarine in a large skillet over medium-high heat, and add the chopped leek. Cook for about 1 minute, stirring occasionally. Reduce the heat, if necessary, to keep the butter from burning. Lay the chicken on top of the leeks. Cook the chicken until both the chicken and the leeks brown (about 5 to 6 minutes). Turn the chicken and cook an additional 3 minutes.

Transfer the chicken to a platter, and cover with foil to keep warm. Add the wine to the skillet and boil, stirring occasionally over medium-high heat, until the liquid is reduced by half (about 2 to 3 minutes).

Arrange the chicken on 4 individual plates, and spoon the sauce over each chicken breast. Serve immediately.

Serves 4

Per serving: 314 calories, 22 g protein, 18 g carbohydrate, 15 g total fat (8 g saturated), 85 mg cholesterol, 442 mg sodium, 272 mg potassium

Baked Chicken and Vegetables

Chicken breasts in this recipe create their own sauce as they bake in individual foil packets. As a timesaver, prepare the packets several hours ahead, and refrigerate them until ready to bake. While the chicken bakes, prepare Rice Pilaf (page 148).

4 medium, skinless, boneless chicken breast halves (1 pound)
8 ounces fresh button mushrooms
6 to 12 green onions, chopped (about ½ cup)

•••

Butter or margarine

•••

¼ cup soy sauce
2 tablespoons lemon juice
2 teaspoons Dijon-style mustard
1 teaspoon snipped fresh tarragon or ¼ teaspoon dried tarragon, crushed
½ to 1 cup all-purpose flour
¼ cup butter or margarine, melted

Rinse the chicken breasts in cold water; pat dry with paper towels. Set aside.

Slice 4 of the mushrooms into thin slices and set aside. Finely chop the remaining mushrooms, and place them in a large bowl. Reserve 2 tablespoons of the chopped green onions; combine the remaining chopped green onions with the chopped mushrooms.

Butter 4 pieces of aluminum foil, each large enough for a chicken breast. Mound equal portions of the mushroom and onion mixture on each piece of foil.

In a medium bowl, combine the soy sauce, lemon juice, mustard, and tarragon. Place the flour on a plate. Dip each chicken breast in the soy mixture, and coat generously with the flour. Place on top of the mushroom mixture. Arrange the reserved sliced mushrooms on top of the chicken. Sprinkle chicken with the reserved onion. Spoon the remaining soy mixture equally over the chicken, and drizzle chicken with a tablespoon of melted butter or margarine.

Seal each foil packet tightly, and bake in a 350° oven for 30 to 35 minutes or until chicken is tender and no longer pink. (The packets can be made ahead and refrigerated for up to 8 hours. If refrigerated, bake an additional 5 to 10 minutes.)

Serves 4

Per serving: 340 calories, 31 g protein, 19 g carbohydrate, 16 g total fat (8 g saturated), 103 mg cholesterol, 1,292 mg sodium, 521 mg potassium

Garlic Chicken

The aroma and rich, sweet taste of cooked garlic enhances the flavor of braised chicken breasts.

8 large cloves garlic, peeled and sliced in half
2 tablespoons olive oil

•••

¼ cup all-purpose flour
½ teaspoon salt
4 medium skinless, boneless chicken breast halves (1 pound)

•••

½ cup dry white wine
½ cup chicken broth
1 teaspoon snipped fresh tarragon or ¼ teaspoon dried tarragon, crushed
2 tablespoons snipped fresh parsley

In a large skillet over medium-low heat, slowly brown the garlic in the olive oil, turning often. Remove the garlic from the skillet and set aside. Reserve pan drippings.

In a shallow bowl, combine the flour and salt. Rinse the chicken and pat dry with paper towels. Lightly coat chicken with flour mixture, shaking off excess. In the skillet, brown the chicken breasts in the reserved pan drippings over medium-high heat for about 1 to 2 minutes on each side.

Return the garlic to the skillet, and add the white wine, chicken broth and tarragon. When the liquids begin to simmer, cover the skillet tightly and reduce the heat to low. Simmer for 10 to 15 minutes or until chicken is tender and no pink remains.

Transfer the chicken to a platter and keep warm. Raise the heat to medium-high, and boil the sauce until it is reduced by about ⅓ (2 to 3 minutes). Stir in the parsley, and pour the sauce over the chicken.

Serves 4

Per serving: 270 calories, 28 g protein, 8 g carbohydrate, 11 g total fat (2 g saturated), 72 mg cholesterol, 432 mg sodium, 302 mg potassium

Chicken with Green Peppercorn Sauce

The piquant flavor of green peppercorns in a rich mustard cream sauce livens up sautéed chicken breasts. If you prefer, bone your own chicken breasts, leaving the skin on for a crispy, golden topping.

4 **skinless, boneless chicken breast halves (1 pound)**
2 **tablespoons butter or margarine**

⚫⚫⚫

½ **cup whipping cream**
2 **teaspoons green peppercorns, rinsed and drained**
½ **teaspoon Dijon-style mustard**
1 **clove garlic, minced**
  Dash salt

Rinse the chicken in cold water and pat dry with paper towels. Melt the butter or margarine in a large skillet, and cook the chicken breasts over medium heat for 5 to 6 minutes on each side or till chicken is tender and no pink remains.

Remove the chicken from the skillet and keep warm. Add the whipping cream, green peppercorns, mustard, garlic, and salt to the pan drippings, and boil over medium-high heat, stirring frequently, until sauce becomes thickened and bubbly.

Pour the sauce over chicken breasts and serve immediately.

Serves 4

Per serving: 377 calories, 40 g protein, 2 g carbohydrate, 23 g total fat (12 g saturated), 165 mg cholesterol, 219 mg sodium, 347 mg potassium

Sour Cream Chicken with Apple and Onion

Rich and tangy sour cream teams with sweet apple and caramelized onion in an easy-does-it meal cooked in foil packets, which make cleanup a snap.

3 tablespoons butter or margarine
1 large onion, thinly sliced
2 small tart red apples, sliced into thin
   wedges

•••

Butter or margarine
4 medium skinless, boneless chicken
   breast halves (1 pound)
Salt
½ cup dairy sour cream
1 teaspoon dried basil or savory,
   crushed

Melt the butter or margarine in a large skillet over low heat, and add the sliced onion. Cook slowly, turning the onion occasionally until tender and caramelized (about 15 to 20 minutes). Add the apple, cover, and cook for about 3 minutes more or just until the apple is soft. Remove the skillet from the heat and set aside.

Butter 4 pieces of aluminum foil, each large enough for a chicken breast. Rinse the chicken breasts in cold water and pat dry with paper towels. Sprinkle with salt. Spread 1 tablespoon of the sour cream on one side of each chicken breast. Place each chicken breast, sour cream side down, on a piece of foil. Spread another tablespoon of sour cream on top of each chicken breast. Sprinkle each with ⅛ teaspoon of the basil or savory. Spoon some of the apple and onion mixture on top of each chicken breast. Seal the foil tightly, making small packets.

Bake packets in a 350° oven for 30 to 35 minutes. To serve, remove the chicken from foil, place on plates, and pour juices over top.

Serves 4

Per serving: 329 calories, 28 g protein, 12 g carbohydrate, 19 g total fat (10 g saturated), 108 mg cholesterol, 201 mg sodium, 367 mg potassium

Chicken with Brandy Sauce

Rice Pilaf (page 148) or Wild and Brown Rice Pilaf (page 149) are good accompaniments for these sautéed chicken breasts topped with a rich brandy and cream sauce. A green vegetable provides a natural garnish.

4 medium skinless, boneless chicken
    breast halves (1 pound)
2 tablespoons butter or margarine

•••

¼ cup brandy
⅛ teaspoon salt
   Dash pepper

•••

½ cup whipping cream
   Dash salt
   Dash pepper

Rinse the chicken breasts in cold water and pat dry with paper towels. Place the chicken breasts between 2 sheets of waxed paper or plastic wrap. With the smooth side of a meat mallet, pound gently to ¼-inch thickness.

Melt the butter or margarine in a large skillet over medium-high heat. Add the chicken breasts, and cook 3 to 5 minutes on each side or until chicken is tender and no pink remains.

Remove the skillet from the heat. Pour the brandy over chicken. Using a long match, immediately ignite the brandy, shaking the skillet gently until the flame dies. Lift the chicken from the pan juices and keep warm. Sprinkle with ⅛ teaspoon salt and a dash of pepper.

Return the skillet to the heat. Add the whipping cream, a dash of salt, and a dash of pepper; boil rapidly over medium-high heat, stirring frequently, until sauce turns golden and shiny bubbles appear (about 2 minutes). Pour over chicken.

Serves 4

Per serving: 333 calories, 27 g protein, 1 g carbohydrate, 21 g total fat (12 g saturated), 129 mg cholesterol, 202 mg sodium, 234 mg potassium

Chicken Gruyère

The addition of sautéed onions and Gruyère cheese adds a "gourmet touch" to this easy and delicious chicken casserole.

3 tablespoons butter or margarine
1 onion, thinly sliced into rings

•••

1 cup shredded Gruyère cheese
    (4 ounces)
¾ cup corn bread stuffing mix
1 teaspoon paprika
4 medium skinless, boneless chicken
    breast halves (1 pound)
    Salt
    Pepper

•••

½ cup dry white wine
½ cup chicken broth
2 tablespoons butter or margarine

Melt 3 tablespoons of butter or margarine in a large skillet. Add the onion; cover and cook slowly until soft but not brown. Remove skillet from heat.

Mix the cheese, stuffing mix, and paprika together. Rinse the chicken breasts in cold water and pat dry with paper towels. Lightly sprinkle the chicken breasts with salt and pepper.

Spread half of the cooked onion in the bottom of a 2-quart square baking dish. Add the chicken breasts, and top with the remaining onion. Cover with the cheese and stuffing mixture. Combine the white wine and chicken broth, and pour over casserole. Dot with 2 tablespoons of butter or margarine.

Bake, uncovered, in a 350° oven for 35 to 40 minutes or until the topping is bubbly and lightly browned and the chicken is tender and no pink remains. Let stand for 10 minutes before serving.

Serves 4

Per serving: 564 calories, 48 g protein, 19 g carbohydrate, 30 g total fat (9 g saturated), 131 mg cholesterol, 709 mg sodium, 453 mg potassium

Chicken with Basil-Orange Sauce

This wonderfully fresh-tasting sauce is worth the extra effort of squeezing your own orange juice. Complete the meal with a mixed green salad or steamed vegetable.

4 medium, skinless, boneless chicken
    breast halves (1 pound)
  Salt
3 tablespoons butter or margarine

•••

6 ounces fettuccine or wide egg noodles

•••

¼ cup finely chopped onion
2 cloves garlic, minced
1 cup freshly squeezed orange juice
    (3 to 4 medium oranges)
1 tablespoon finely shredded orange
    peel
1 tablespoon snipped fresh basil or
    1 teaspoon dried basil, crushed

•••

  Orange slices
  Fresh basil or parsley

Rinse chicken breasts in cold water; pat dry with paper towels. Sprinkle with salt to taste. In a skillet, melt butter or margarine over medium heat. Cook chicken for 3 to 5 minutes on each side. Reduce heat slightly if butter begins to burn. Transfer chicken to a platter, and cover with foil to keep warm. Meanwhile, cook fettuccine or noodles according to package directions.

Add the onion and garlic to the pan drippings, and cook over low heat for 2 to 3 minutes or until soft. Add the orange juice, orange peel, and basil. Raise the heat to high and boil, stirring occasionally, for about 5 minutes or until the sauce is reduced by about half. Toss 2 to 3 tablespoons of the orange-basil sauce with the hot cooked fettuccine or noodles. Divide the fettuccine or noodles among 4 serving plates. Top with the chicken and remaining sauce. Garnish with orange slices and fresh basil or parsley.

Serves 4

Per serving: 387 calories, 27 g protein, 38 g carbohydrate, 14 g total fat (6 g saturated), 145 mg cholesterol, 189 mg sodium, 424 mg potassium

Blue Cheese Chicken Rolls

The combination of blue, Swiss, and cream cheeses makes a rich filling for these rolled chicken breasts.

6 large skinless, boneless chicken breast
   halves (1¾ pounds)

• • •

2 3-ounce packages cream cheese,
   softened
1 ounce blue cheese, crumbled
1 ounce Swiss cheese, shredded
   (¼ cup)

• • •

⅓ cup all-purpose flour
2 beaten eggs
1 cup crushed blue cheese-flavored
   crackers or rich round crackers
¼ cup butter or margarine, melted

Rinse the chicken breasts in cold water; pat dry with paper towels. Place the chicken breasts between 2 sheets of waxed paper or plastic wrap. With the flat side of a meat mallet, pound gently to ¼-inch thickness.

Combine the cream cheese, blue cheese, and Swiss cheese. Spread about 2 tablespoons of the cheese mixture on each chicken breast.

Starting at one end, roll up each chicken breast, folding in sides to seal tightly. Coat each chicken roll lightly with flour, dip in beaten eggs, and roll in the crushed crackers.

Place the chicken rolls in a shallow baking dish. Drizzle with melted butter or margarine. Bake in a 400° oven for 35 to 40 minutes or until chicken is tender and no pink remains.

Serves 6

Per serving: 456 calories, 35 g protein, 14 g carbohydrate, 29 g total fat (11 g saturated), 182 mg cholesterol, 409 mg sodium, 287 mg potassium

Chicken Tarragon with Mushrooms

The very French combination of tarragon, chicken, and mushrooms deserves the very French accompaniment of Potatoes Parisian (page 140) and, "but of course," a fresh, crusty loaf of French bread (page 182).

4 medium skinless, boneless chicken
   breast halves (1 pound)
2 tablespoons butter or margarine

•••

1½ cups sliced fresh mushrooms
½ cup sliced green onions

•••

¾ cup dry white wine
2 teaspoons snipped fresh parsley
½ teaspoon dried tarragon, crushed, or
   2 teaspoons snipped fresh tarragon

Rinse the chicken; pat dry with paper towels. Melt the butter or margarine in a large skillet over medium-high heat. Quickly brown the chicken breasts on both sides.

Remove the chicken from the skillet. Add the mushrooms and green onions and cook until onions are tender and mushrooms are golden.

Return chicken to the skillet. Add the wine, parsley, and tarragon. Bring to a boil, reduce heat, and cover pan. Simmer over low heat about 12 minutes or until chicken is tender and no pink remains.

Place the chicken breasts on a serving dish, and pour the wine-vegetable mixture over the chicken.

Serves 4

Per serving: 202 calories, 21 g protein, 3 g carbohydrate, 9 g total fat (4 g saturated), 70 mg cholesterol, 113 mg sodium, 324 mg potassium

Swiss Chicken Supreme

When serving, garnish this easy-bake chicken casserole with a few fresh raspberries and sprigs of parsley.

4 medium skinless, boneless chicken breast halves (1 pound)

Marinade:

1 tablespoon raspberry vinegar
2 green onions, chopped (¼ cup)
⅛ teaspoon salt
⅛ teaspoon pepper
3 tablespoons olive oil

···

2 cups fresh white bread crumbs (about 2½ slices)
½ cup shredded Swiss cheese (2 ounces)
½ teaspoon dried marjoram, crushed, or 2 teaspoons snipped fresh marjoram
½ teaspoon dried thyme, crushed, or 2 teaspoons snipped fresh thyme
2 tablespoons butter or margarine, melted

Rinse the chicken; pat dry with paper towels. Place the chicken breasts in a 2-quart square baking dish.

Marinade: In a small bowl, combine the raspberry vinegar, green onions, salt, and pepper. Whisk in the olive oil. Pour over chicken, and marinate at room temperature for 10 minutes, turning once.

Combine the bread crumbs, cheese, marjoram, and thyme. Cover the chicken and marinade with the bread-crumb mixture. Drizzle with melted butter or margarine. Bake in a 350° oven for 35 to 40 minutes or until the chicken is tender and no pink remains and the topping is golden.

Serves 4

Per serving: 367 calories, 26 g protein, 13 g carbohydrate, 23 g total fat (8 g saturated), 83 mg cholesterol, 327 mg sodium, 221 mg potassium

Chicken in Port Sauce

Slowly simmering chicken in port wine and herbes de Provence brings a delicate but succulent flavor to this elegant recipe. Clarified butter—butter with the milk solids removed—does not burn easily, making it a good choice for browning the chicken.

**2 to 2½ pounds meaty chicken pieces
    (breasts, thighs, drumsticks)**
5 tablespoons butter
Salt
**½ cup finely chopped shallots
    (about 4 large shallots)**
1 teaspoon herbes de Provence
1 cup port wine

Remove the skin from the chicken pieces, if desired. Rinse chicken in cold water; pat dry with paper towels.

Clarify the butter: Melt butter in a small pan without stirring; pour into a small, narrow glass. After it stands for about 3 minutes, remove the floating foam from the top with a spoon. Measure 2 tablespoons of the clear liquid, and discard the whey at the bottom of the glass.

Heat the clarified butter in a large skillet over medium-high heat. When hot enough to sizzle, add the chicken pieces (do not crowd), and brown on all sides. Transfer chicken pieces to a platter. Sprinkle chicken lightly with salt. Pour off all but 1 tablespoon of fat from the skillet. Lower the heat to medium. Add the chopped shallots, and cook for about 1 minute, stirring often. Return the chicken pieces to the skillet. Add the herbes de Provence and port wine. Cover skillet tightly, and reduce the heat to low. Simmer for 30 to 40 minutes or until the chicken is tender and no pink remains.

To serve, pour cooking liquid over chicken.

Serves 4

Per serving: 432 calories, 32 g protein, 10 g carbohydrate, 22 g total fat (11 g saturated), 133 mg cholesterol, 367 mg sodium, 333 mg potassium

Cinnamon-Orange Chicken

Cinnamon and cloves aren't used just in desserts. These spices give a rich, reddish brown color and exotic flavor to chicken that is simmered in orange juice with raisins.

2 to 2½ pounds meaty chicken pieces
  (breasts, thighs, drumsticks)

• • •

¼ cup all-purpose flour
1 tablespoon ground cinnamon
1 teaspoon ground cloves
½ teaspoon salt

• • •

2 tablespoons butter or margarine
2 tablespoons olive oil

• • •

1 onion, chopped
1 cup orange juice
¼ cup golden raisins

• • •

Hot cooked rice
Parsley sprigs
Orange slices

Remove the skin from the chicken pieces, if desired. Rinse chicken in cold water; pat dry with paper towels.

Combine the flour, cinnamon, cloves, and salt. Lightly coat the chicken pieces in the flour mixture, and shake off excess.

Heat the butter or margarine and olive oil in a large skillet over medium heat. When hot, add the chicken pieces, and brown on all sides. Remove the chicken from the skillet.

Add the chopped onion and cook, stirring frequently, until onion is tender and begins to brown. Return the chicken pieces to the skillet. Add the orange juice and raisins. Cover and reduce heat to low. Simmer for 30 to 40 minutes or until chicken is tender.

Remove the chicken from the skillet and keep warm. Increase the heat to high, and boil remaining pan juices rapidly, stirring occasionally, until sauce reduces and thickens slightly (about 4 to 5 minutes).

Serve chicken with hot cooked rice. Top with the sauce and garnish with parsley and orange slices.

Serves 4

Per serving: 650 calories, 40 g protein, 53 g carbohydrate, 31 g total fat (10 g saturated), 128 mg cholesterol, 435 mg sodium, 577 mg potassium

Casbah Chicken

Three signature spices of North African cooking—cinnamon, cumin, and cayenne pepper—flavor a citrus sauce. If you plan to use freshly squeezed orange juice, you will need three or four medium oranges for 1 cup of juice.

Orange Basmati Rice:

- 1 cup basmati or other long-grain rice
- 2 cups cold water
- 2 teaspoons instant chicken bouillon granules
- 1 tablespoon finely shredded orange peel
- ¼ teaspoon salt

•••

- 4 medium skinless, boneless chicken breast halves (1 pound)
- Salt
- 2 tablespoons butter or margarine

•••

- ¼ cup chopped green onion
- 2 teaspoons finely shredded orange peel
- 1 cup orange juice
- 1 tablespoon brown sugar
- ¼ teaspoon ground cinnamon
- ¼ teaspoon ground cumin
- Dash to ⅛ teaspoon cayenne pepper
- 2 tablespoons golden or dark raisins, coarsely chopped

•••

- Fresh cilantro sprigs
- Orange slices

Orange Basmati Rice: In a 1 ½-quart saucepan, bring the water to a boil over high heat. Add the rice, chicken bouillon, 1 tablespoon orange peel, and ¼ teaspoon salt. Return to boiling, stir, and cover. Reduce heat to low, and cook for 15 minutes or until liquid is absorbed. Remove from the heat, and keep covered until ready to serve.

Rinse the chicken in cold water; pat dry with paper towels. Lightly sprinkle chicken with salt.

Melt the butter or margarine in a skillet over medium heat. Cook the chicken for 4 to 5 minutes on each side or till chicken is tender and no pink remains. Remove chicken from skillet; keep warm.

Add the green onion to the pan drippings, and cook over low heat for 1 minute, stirring frequently. Add the orange peel, orange juice, brown sugar, cinnamon, cumin, cayenne pepper, and raisins to the skillet. Raise the heat to medium high. Boil, stirring frequently, for about 5 minutes or until sauce is reduced by half.

Fluff the rice and divide among 4 individual plates. Arrange the chicken breasts on top of the rice, and spoon the sauce over the chicken. Garnish with fresh cilantro and orange slices.

Serves 4

Per serving: 391 calories, 24 g protein, 51 g carbohydrate, 9 g total fat (5 g saturated), 70 mg cholesterol, 696 mg sodium, 408 mg potassium

Chicken Caribe

A flavorful spice blend coats the chicken breasts, which then simmer in a sauce of fresh tomato, lime juice, and crushed red pepper.

Spice Blend:

- 1 teaspoon ground cumin
- 1 teaspoon ground coriander
- ½ teaspoon chili powder
- ¼ teaspoon salt

•••

- 4 medium skinless, boneless chicken breast halves (1 pound)
- 2 tablespoons olive oil

•••

- 4 green onions, chopped
- 4 cloves garlic, minced
- 2 tomatoes, peeled and chopped
- 2 tablespoons lime juice
- ½ teaspoon crushed red pepper
- Salt
- Pepper

•••

- Hot cooked rice

Spice Blend: In a small bowl combine the cumin, coriander, chili powder, and salt.

Rinse the chicken; pat dry with paper towels. Sprinkle spice blend evenly over both sides of the chicken breasts. Heat the olive oil in a large skillet over medium-high heat. Brown the chicken breasts in hot oil (about 1 minute per side). Transfer them to a platter and set aside.

Reduce the heat to medium-low, and fry the onion and garlic for about 1 minute. Return the chicken to the pan. Add the tomatoes, lime juice, and red pepper. Add salt and pepper to taste. Cover the skillet tightly, and simmer the chicken over medium-low heat for 8 to 10 minutes or until tender and no pink remains. Remove the chicken from the skillet; keep warm.

Raise the heat to medium-high and simmer the sauce to reduce it by about half, stirring frequently (5 minutes).

To serve, place the chicken on a bed of rice, and spoon the sauce over the top.

Serves 4

Per serving: 372 calories, 30 g protein, 36 g carbohydrate, 12 g total fat (2 g saturated), 72 mg cholesterol, 213 mg sodium, 505 mg potassium

Bayou Chicken

The jazzy flavors of Louisiana cooking make this oven-fried chicken a spicy favorite. It's a welcome alternative to the usual fried chicken at picnics and potluck parties. If you're crushing your own corn flakes, start with 3 cups to yield 1½ cups crushed.

2 to 2½ pounds meaty chicken pieces
(breasts, thighs, drumsticks)

Coating:
1½ cups cornflake crumbs
1 tablespoon paprika
2 teaspoons garlic powder
1 teaspoon onion powder
1 teaspoon dried thyme, crushed
1 teaspoon snipped fresh parsley
1 teaspoon dried oregano, crushed
1 teaspoon salt
1 teaspoon black pepper
½ teaspoon cayenne pepper

• • •

1 beaten egg
½ cup milk

• • •

3 tablespoons butter or margarine,
melted

Remove the skin from the chicken pieces, if desired. Rinse chicken in cold water; pat dry with paper towels.

In a large bowl, combine the cornflake crumbs with the paprika, garlic powder, onion powder, thyme, parsley, oregano, salt, black pepper, and cayenne pepper. In a separate bowl, combine the egg and milk. Dip the chicken pieces in the egg mixture, then roll them in the crumb mixture.

Grease a 3-quart rectangular baking dish. Arrange the chicken pieces in the baking dish, bone side down. Drizzle with melted butter or margarine and bake, uncovered, for 45 to 55 minutes in a 375° oven or until chicken is tender and no pink remains.

Serves 4

Per serving: 454 calories, 39 g protein, 10 g carbohydrate, 28 g total fat (11 g saturated), 191 mg cholesterol, 822 mg sodium, 416 mg potassium

Chicken Chilaquiles

A Mexican casserole layered with corn tortillas, chicken, Monterey jack cheese, and salsa tastes great with a refreshing margarita. Start the meal with Lime Soup (page 135).

3 bone-in chicken breast halves (1½ pounds) or 2 cups chopped cooked chicken
1 cup vegetable oil or shortening
10 6-inch corn tortillas
½ cup finely chopped onion
2 cloves garlic, minced

•••

1 16-ounce jar salsa or 2 cups Tomato Salsa (page 196)
Salt
½ cup dairy sour cream
1½ cups shredded Monterey jack cheese (6 ounces)

•••

2 tablespoons snipped fresh cilantro
Additional salsa (optional)

If using chicken breasts, rinse them in cold water. Cook the chicken breasts in boiling water; drain and cool. Remove the skin and bones, and cut into ¾-inch pieces (should have about 2 cups).

Heat the vegetable oil or shortening in a saucepan or skillet. With a pair of tongs, dip each tortilla in the hot oil to soften. Do this quickly or the tortillas will harden. Drain on paper towels. When cool, slice the tortillas into quarters.

In a small bowl, combine the chopped onion and garlic.

To assemble: Put a small amount of salsa in the bottom of a 2-quart square baking dish and cover with ¼ of the quartered tortillas; salt lightly. Spread ¼ of the sour cream on top of the tortillas. Sprinkle with ⅓ of the onion-garlic mixture and the chicken. Top with ¼ of the shredded cheese. Spoon some of the salsa over all. Repeat with the remaining ingredients, ending with a layer of tortillas, salsa, and cheese.

Bake, uncovered, in a 350° oven for 30 minutes or until the cheese melts and the casserole is bubbly. Remove the casserole from the oven and immediately sprinkle with cilantro leaves. Let stand for 10 minutes before cutting. If desired, pass additional salsa when serving.

Serves 6

Per serving: 452 calories, 26 g protein, 32 g carbohydrate, 25 g total fat (9 g saturated), 74 mg cholesterol, 811 mg sodium, 435 mg potassium

Fajita Lasagne

Toasting the cumin seed and oregano greatly intensifies the flavor of the spice mixture. Place the cumin seed or oregano in a small skillet over low heat. Stir constantly until the herb is light brown. It will take about 2 minutes for the cumin seed and about 1 minute for the oregano. Watch the herbs carefully so they don't burn.

Spice Mixture:
- 1 teaspoon toasted cumin seed, crushed
- 1 teaspoon chili powder
- ¼ teaspoon toasted dried oregano, crushed
- ¼ teaspoon salt
- ¼ teaspoon ground cinnamon
- ⅛ teaspoon ground cloves
- ⅛ teaspoon pepper

•••

- 6 ounces skinless, boneless chicken breast halves, sliced into thin strips
- 2 tablespoons olive oil or vegetable oil
- 1 small onion, thinly sliced
- 1 green sweet pepper, coarsely chopped
- 1 red sweet pepper, coarsely chopped
- 3 cloves garlic, finely chopped
- 1 tablespoon lime juice

Cilantro Sour Cream:
- ½ cup dairy sour cream
- 2 tablespoons snipped fresh cilantro
- 1 clove garlic, minced

•••

- 1 cup chunky salsa
- 4 large flour tortillas
- 1½ cups shredded Monterey jack cheese (6 ounces)
- 2 tablespoons snipped fresh cilantro

Spice Mixture: In a small bowl, combine the cumin, chili powder, oregano, salt, cinnamon, cloves, and pepper.

Rinse the chicken; pat dry with paper towels. In a large skillet, heat the oil over medium heat. Add the onion, green and red sweet peppers, and garlic. Stir-fry for 2 to 3 minutes or until peppers are crisp-tender. Add the chicken, sprinkle with the spice mixture, and stir-fry for 2 to 3 minutes more or till chicken is no longer pink. Stir in the lime juice. Let the mixture cool slightly.

Cilantro Sour Cream: In a small bowl, combine sour cream, cilantro, and garlic. Let stand for 5 minutes.

To assemble: Grease a 2-quart square baking dish. Place a tortilla on the bottom of the dish. Spread ⅓ of the Cilantro Sour Cream evenly over tortilla. Spread ¼ of the salsa over the sour cream layer. Spoon about ⅓ of the chicken fajita mixture on top. Sprinkle with ¼ of the cheese. Repeat layers twice. Top with the remaining tortilla, salsa, and cheese.

Bake, uncovered, in a 350° oven for 20 to 25 minutes or until heated through. Remove from the oven and immediately sprinkle with the cilantro. Let rest for 10 minutes before cutting.

Serves 4

Per serving: 561 calories, 27 g protein, 42 g carbohydrate, 31 g total fat (14 g saturated), 78 mg cholesterol, 1067 mg sodium, 454 mg potassium

Island Chicken Rolls with Pineapple Sauce

For an impressive presentation, slice these chicken breasts before serving to reveal the tempting filling of shrimp, cheese, and macadamia nuts.

4 medium skinless, boneless chicken breast halves (1 pound)
2 cups water
12 medium shrimp, shelled and deveined
¼ cup shredded Gouda cheese (1 ounce)
2 tablespoons macadamia nuts, coarsely chopped

• • •

⅓ cup fine dry bread crumbs
¼ cup unsweetened shredded or flaked coconut

• • •

¼ cup butter or margarine, melted

Pineapple Sauce:
1 8-ounce can pineapple tidbits (juice pack)
½ teaspoon cornstarch

Rinse the chicken in cold water and pat dry with paper towels. Place each chicken breast half between 2 sheets of waxed paper or plastic wrap. Pound gently with the flat side of a meat mallet to ¼-inch thickness.

Bring the water to a rolling boil in a medium saucepan. Add the shelled and deveined shrimp, and remove the pan from the heat. Wait 30 seconds, then drain shrimp well.

In a small bowl, combine the Gouda cheese and macadamia nuts. In another bowl, combine the bread crumbs and coconut.

Place 3 shrimp in the center of each chicken breast half. Sprinkle equal amounts of the cheese and nut mixture over the halves. Starting at one end, roll up the chicken half, folding in the sides to seal tightly. Secure with wooden toothpicks. Dip each chicken roll in the melted butter or margarine and roll in the bread-crumb-and-coconut mixture.

Place the chicken rolls in a 2-quart square baking dish. Drizzle with any remaining butter or margarine. Bake, uncovered, in a 400° oven for 30 to 35 minutes or until lightly browned and no pink remains.

Pineapple Sauce: Drain juice from pineapple into a small saucepan. Add cornstarch and blend thoroughly. Cook over medium heat, stirring constantly, until the juice thickens slightly and bubbles. Add the pineapple tidbits and heat through. Serve the sauce over the chicken rolls.

Serves 4

Per serving: 387 calories, 33 g protein, 16 g carbohydrate, 21 g total fat (5 g saturated), 105 mg cholesterol, 328 mg sodium, 350 mg potassium

Spicy North African Chicken

The spicy trio of cinnamon, cumin, and cayenne pepper enhances the flavor of this roasted chicken. A flavorful white wine sauce made from the pan drippings is served over the chicken.

1 2½- to 3-pound broiler-fryer chicken, quartered

Marinade:
¼ cup orange juice
1 tablespoon lemon juice
1 teaspoon ground cumin
1 teaspoon ground coriander
½ teaspoon salt
½ teaspoon ground cinnamon
¼ to ½ teaspoon ground red pepper
2 tablespoons snipped fresh cilantro
2 cloves garlic, minced
3 tablespoons olive oil

•••

¼ cup dry white wine

•••

Fresh cilantro sprigs
Orange slices

Rinse the chicken quarters in cold water and pat dry with paper towels. Twist the wing tips under the back.

Marinade: In a small bowl, combine orange juice, lemon juice, cumin, coriander, salt, cinnamon, red pepper, cilantro, garlic, and olive oil. Place the chicken quarters in a large shallow dish, and pour the marinade over them. Cover and marinate in the refrigerator for 4 to 24 hours, turning the chicken several times in the marinade.

Place a rack in a shallow roasting pan. Place the chicken on the rack, skin side up. Roast the chicken in a 375° oven for 50 to 60 minutes or until the joints move easily and the juices run clear. Baste the chicken with the remaining marinade several times while cooking. (Do not baste the chicken during the last 10 minutes of roasting.) Remove the chicken from the pan; cover and keep warm.

Skim the fat from the pan juices and discard. Pour the juices into a small saucepan. Add the dry white wine. Simmer the sauce gently over medium heat until it is reduced by about a third (3 to 4 minutes).

To serve, spoon some of the sauce over each piece of chicken. Garnish with cilantro and orange slices.

Serves 4

Per serving: 419 calories, 35 g protein, 3 g carbohydrate, 28 g total fat (6 g saturated), 113 mg cholesterol, 373 mg sodium, 356 mg potassium

Chicken India

While the chicken bakes, prepare packaged couscous or rice to serve with this saucy meal.

4 medium, skinless, boneless chicken breast halves (1 pound)

Spice Mixture:

1 tablespoon butter or margarine, melted
1 tablespoon lemon juice
½ teaspoon salt
½ teaspoon ground ginger
½ teaspoon ground coriander
¼ teaspoon ground cardamom
¼ teaspoon coarsely ground pepper
¼ teaspoon chili powder
⅛ teaspoon ground cloves

• • •

1 tablespoon butter or margarine
1 cup finely chopped onion
⅛ teaspoon saffron threads, crushed (optional)
¾ cup whipping cream
3 tablespoons sliced almonds
2 tablespoons raisins, coarsely chopped

Rinse the chicken; pat dry with paper towels. Place the chicken in a 9x9x2-inch baking pan.

Spice Mixture: In a small bowl, combine the 1 tablespoon melted butter or margarine, lemon juice, salt, ginger, coriander, cardamom, pepper, chili powder, and cloves. Brush the mixture on both sides of the chicken.

Melt 1 tablespoon butter or margarine in a skillet. Add the onion, and cook over medium heat until golden brown. Stir in the saffron, if desired. Add the whipping cream, almonds, and raisins. Bring the mixture to a boil over medium-high heat. Boil, stirring frequently, for 2 to 3 minutes or until the sauce thickens slightly. Pour the sauce evenly over the chicken.

Bake, uncovered, in a 350° oven for 25 to 30 minutes or until the chicken is tender and no pink remains.

Place chicken breasts on individual plates. Stir sauce in dish and spoon over the chicken.

Serves 4

Per serving: 375 calories, 22 g protein, 11 g carbohydrate, 28 g total fat (15 g saturated), 131 mg cholesterol, 395 mg sodium, 343 mg potassium

Chicken Curry

To toast the almonds (or other nuts), place them in a shallow baking pan and bake in a 350° oven for 5 to 10 minutes or until light golden brown.

12 ounces skinless, boneless chicken
   breast halves

•••

¼ cup butter or margarine
1 cup chopped onion, chopped
2 cloves garlic, minced

•••

1 tart red apple, cored and chopped
   into ½-inch pieces
2 tablespoons raisins, chopped

•••

3 tablespoons all-purpose flour
1 to 2 tablespoons curry powder
1½ cups chicken broth

•••

½ cup plain yogurt

•••

3 cups hot cooked rice
½ cup slivered almonds, toasted

Rinse the chicken; pat dry with paper towels. Cut the chicken into 1-inch pieces and set aside.

Melt the butter or margarine in a large skillet over medium-low heat. Add the onion and garlic and cook, stirring frequently, until golden (5 to 6 minutes).

Add the chicken, apple, and raisins. Cook, stirring frequently, for 3 to 5 minutes or until chicken is tender and no pink remains. Stir in the flour and curry powder, and cook for 1 minute more. Slowly stir in the chicken broth; cook and stir till thickened and bubbly, then cook and stir for 1 minute more.

Stir in the yogurt; heat through, but do not let the mixture boil.

Serve the chicken curry over rice, and garnish with toasted almonds.

Serves 4

Per serving: 489 calories, 29 g protein, 40 g carbohydrate, 25 g total fat (9 g saturated), 87 mg cholesterol, 553 mg sodium, 621 mg potassium

Prize Catches

Be sure your catch of the day is prepared just the way you like it. Whether you're searching for entrée or salad recipes, our fish chapter will reel you in.

Shrimp Salad with Coriander-Lime Dressing

Serve this festive south-of-the-border salad with your favorite Mexican entrée. Two medium fresh oranges, peeled and sectioned, may be substituted for the mandarin oranges.

8 ounces shrimp with shells

Coriander-Lime Dressing:

1 tablespoon red wine vinegar
1 tablespoon lime juice
2 cloves garlic, minced
½ teaspoon sugar
½ teaspoon ground coriander
½ teaspoon chili powder
½ cup olive oil

•••

1 large head leaf lettuce, rinsed and
   chilled
2 green onions, chopped
1 avocado, pitted, peeled, and sliced
1 11-ounce can mandarin oranges,
   drained

In a large saucepan, bring 3 quarts water to boiling. Add the shrimp and cook for 3 to 5 minutes or until the shrimp turn pink. Rinse the shrimp in cold water and drain. Shell and devein the shrimp. Cover and chill until serving time.

Coriander-Lime Dressing: In a small bowl, combine the vinegar, lime juice, garlic, sugar, coriander, and chili powder. Whisk in the olive oil.

To assemble: Tear the lettuce leaves, and place them in a large salad bowl. Add the chilled shrimp, green onions, avocado, and oranges. Whisk the salad dressing and pour desired amount over the salad. Toss gently and arrange salad on plates.

Serves 4 to 6

Per serving: 409 calories, 12 g protein, 15 g carbohydrate, 36 g total fat (5 g saturated), 83 mg cholesterol, 115 mg sodium, 688 mg potassium

Scallops with Bacon and Sherry

About 20 minutes is all you'll need to prepare this sophisticated entrée.

3 strips bacon
1 cup sliced fresh mushrooms

•••

1 pound bay scallops
3 green onions, chopped
½ teaspoon dried tarragon or thyme,
    crushed, or 2 teaspoons fresh
    snipped tarragon or thyme
¼ cup dry sherry

•••

2 teaspoons cornstarch
¼ cup water

•••

Hot cooked rice or linguine

Cook the bacon in a large skillet over medium heat until crisp. Drain the bacon on paper towel, crumble, and set aside. Reserve bacon drippings in skillet.

Add the sliced mushrooms to the bacon drippings. Cook and stir just until tender.

Add the scallops, green onions, tarragon, and sherry. Simmer for 3 to 5 minutes or until the liquid is reduced by half and scallops are opaque.

Combine the cornstarch and water. Add slowly to scallop mixture, stirring until the liquid thickens and bubbles. Cook 1 minute more. Serve with white rice or linguine. Top each serving with some of the crumbled bacon.

Serves 4

Per serving: 377 calories, 24 g protein, 34 g carbohydrate, 14 g total fat (6 g saturated), 52 mg cholesterol, 319 mg sodium, 518 mg potassium

Deluxe Tuna Casserole

Bow tie pasta and the addition of white wine gives this old favorite a classy touch.

1 10-ounce can cream of celery soup
½ cup milk
¼ cup dry white wine
¼ teaspoon salt
¼ teaspoon pepper

•••

1 6⅛-ounce can albacore tuna, drained
1 cup frozen peas
1 cup shredded cheddar cheese
  (4 ounces)
1 tablespoon chopped pimiento

•••

8 ounces bow tie pasta (farfalle) or
  wide egg noodles, cooked and
  drained

In a large bowl, combine the soup, milk, wine, salt, and pepper. Stir in the tuna, peas, cheese, and pimiento. Add the cooked pasta and mix well.

Pour into a greased 2-quart casserole. Cover and bake in a 375° oven for 25 minutes. Uncover the casserole and bake for an additional 10 minutes or until casserole is hot and bubbly.

Serves 4

Per serving: 489 calories, 30 g protein, 52 g carbohydrate, 17 g total fat (7 g saturated), 143 mg cholesterol, 1073 mg sodium, 466 mg potassium

Orange Roughy with Brandy-Lemon Glaze

A glaze of butter, lemon, brandy, and a touch of brown sugar is the perfect topping for delicately flavored fish.

4 orange roughy fillets
    (about 1½ pounds)
¼ cup butter or margarine
3 to 4 tablespoons milk
1 cup cornflake crumbs

Brandy- Lemon Glaze:
2 tablespoons butter or margarine
¼ cup lemon juice
¼ cup brandy
2 tablespoons brown sugar

Rinse fish; pat dry with paper towels.

Melt the butter or margarine in a large skillet. Dip the fish in milk, then in cornflake crumbs. Cook over medium heat for 2 to 4 minutes on each side or until the the fish flakes easily and the coating is golden brown. Remove fish from skillet and keep warm. Reserve pan drippings.

Brandy-Lemon Glaze: To the pan drippings, add the butter or margarine, lemon juice, brandy or chicken broth, and brown sugar. Stir over medium heat until the sugar dissolves. Continue cooking, stirring occasionally, until the mixture begins to caramelize and thicken slightly, (4 to 5 minutes). Pour glaze over fillets and serve immediately.

Serves 4

Per serving: 354 calories, 22 g protein, 17 g carbohydrate, 19 g total fat (11 g saturated), 75 mg cholesterol, 397 mg sodium, 479 mg potassium

Fish with Lemon Cream

Dress your prize catch in a crispy coating and top with a lemony sauce—it's sure to be a blue-ribbon winner.

8 sole, bass, or crappie fillets or other
    fish fillets (about 1 pound)
1 egg, slightly beaten
2 tablespoons milk
1 cup cornflake crumbs
¼ cup butter or margarine

Lemon Cream:
½ cup whipping cream
1 tablespoon lemon juice
1 teaspoon Dijon-style mustard

Rinse the fish fillets; pat dry with paper towels.

Combine the egg and milk. Dip 4 of the fish fillets in the egg mixture, then roll in the cornflake crumbs. Melt 2 tablespoons of the butter or margarine in a large skillet. Cook fish over medium heat for 2 to 3 minutes on each side or until the fish flakes easily and the coating is golden brown. Remove the fish from the skillet and keep warm. Repeat with remaining fish and remaining butter or margarine.

Lemon Cream: In a saucepan, combine the whipping cream, lemon juice, and mustard. Bring to a boil over medium-high heat, stirring frequently. Boil gently for about 5 minutes or until sauce thickens slightly. Pour over fish fillets and serve immediately.

Serves 4

Per serving: 375 calories, 24 g protein, 13 g carbohydrate, 26 g total fat (15 g saturated), 177 mg cholesterol, 392 mg sodium, 381 mg potassium

Oven-Roasted Halibut with Tomato Relish

To easily toast the pine nuts or almonds, place them in a small skillet and cook over medium heat for 2 to 4 minutes, stirring frequently, until the nuts are golden brown.

Tomato Relish:

- 2 tablespoons lemon juice
- 1 tablespoon snipped fresh cilantro
- 2 cloves garlic, minced
- ⅛ teaspoon pepper
- 2 tablespoons olive oil
- ¼ cup finely chopped oil-pack dried tomatoes, well drained
- 2 tablespoons finely chopped pimento-stuffed green olives
- 2 tablespoons finely chopped pitted ripe olives
- 2 tablespoons toasted pine nuts or slivered almonds

•••

- 1 tablespoon olive oil
- 1 pound halibut steaks or fillets
  Salt (optional)

Tomato Relish: In a medium bowl, combine lemon juice, cilantro, garlic, and pepper. Gradually whisk in 2 tablespoons olive oil. Stir in tomatoes, olives, and pine nuts or almonds. Set aside.

Heat 1 tablespoon olive oil in a large skillet. Add fish to skillet and cook for 1 minute or till lightly browned. Transfer to a 2-quart baking dish, browned side up. If desired, sprinkle fish with salt.

Bake, uncovered, in a 450° oven for 4 to 6 minutes per ½-inch thickness of fish or until fish flakes easily with a fork.

To serve, top each serving with some of the relish.

Serves 4

Per serving: 267 calories, 25 g protein, 4 g carbohydrate, 17 g total fat (2 g saturated), 36 mg cholesterol, 180 mg sodium, 667 mg potassium

Fried Salmon Cakes

Need a quick meal? Try this rendition of an old family standard. Choose one of the clever ideas from Vegetable Dress-Ups (page 163) to round out the meal.

1   14¾-ounce can salmon, drained
1   egg, slightly beaten
¾   cup saltine cracker crumbs
        (about 21 crackers)
¼   cup finely chopped onion
¼   teaspoon salt
¼   teaspoon dried dillweed
¼   teaspoon pepper
        •••
2   tablespoons cooking oil

Horseradish Sauce:
½   cup catsup
4   teaspoons horseradish
¼   teaspoon lemon juice
        Dash Worcestershire sauce

Remove the bones and skin from salmon. In a medium bowl, combine the egg, cracker crumbs, onion, salt, dillweed, and pepper. Add the salmon and mix well. Shape into 4 patties, each about 1 inch thick.

Heat the oil in a large skillet. Cook the salmon cakes over medium heat for 3 to 5 minutes on each side or until golden.

Horseradish Sauce: In a small bowl, combine catsup, horseradish, lemon juice, and Worcestershire sauce. Serve with the salmon cakes.

Serves 4

Per serving: 324 calories, 23 g protein, 21 g carbohydrate, 16 g total fat (3 g saturated), 108 mg cholesterol, 1,273 mg sodium, 527 mg potassium

In Your Own Backyard.......

Grilling doesn't have to mean just hamburgers. Try our innovative main dishes, salads, and accompaniments that will mean delightful meals for family and friends.

Smoked Chicken on Pasta with Tomatoes

Chicken breasts smoked on the grill are served atop pasta smothered with a garlic-tomato sauce. If you're using the canned tomatoes, use kitchen scissors to cut up the tomatoes while they are still in the can. This way you won't lose any of the juice.

4 medium skinless, boneless chicken
   breast halves (1 pound)
4 teaspoons olive oil
⅛ teaspoon salt
½ cup apple wood smoking chips

   •••

3 tablespoons olive oil
1 tablespoon finely chopped garlic
   (6 cloves)
4 cups peeled, chopped fresh tomatoes
   or two 14½-ounce cans Italian plum
   tomatoes, undrained and chopped
2 to 3 tablespoons snipped fresh basil or
   1 to 1½ teaspoons dried basil,
   crushed
¼ teaspoon salt
¼ teaspoon crushed red pepper
⅛ teaspoon black pepper

   •••

12 ounces fettuccine or linguine, cooked
¼ cup shredded Parmesan cheese
   Fresh basil leaves

Rinse the chicken breasts in cold water; pat dry with paper towels. Brush with 4 teaspoons olive oil and sprinkle with ⅛ teaspoon salt.

Place the apple wood chips on a 12x10-inch piece of aluminum foil, and seal tightly to make a foil packet. Pierce the foil in several places to allow the smoke to escape.

In a covered grill, arrange medium-hot coals around a drip pan; test for medium heat over the drip pan. Place foil packet on coals. Place chicken breasts on grill rack over drip pan. Cover and grill for 15 to 18 minutes or until chicken is tender and no pink remains. Remove chicken from the grill; keep warm.

Heat 3 tablespoons olive oil in a large skillet over medium heat. Add the garlic. Swirl the skillet or stir the garlic gently until it is golden brown. Add the chopped tomatoes, basil, ¼ teaspoon salt, crushed red pepper, and black pepper. Bring to boiling; reduce heat. Simmer, uncovered, over medium heat for 3 to 4 minutes or until the sauce thickens slightly.

Divide pasta among 4 individual plates; top with sauce. Slice chicken into ½-inch-thick slices, and arrange chicken on top of sauce. Sprinkle with Parmesan cheese and garnish with fresh basil leaves.

Serves 4

Per serving: 629 calories, 35 g protein, 73 g carbohydrate, 22 g total fat (4 g saturated), 77 mg cholesterol, 386 mg sodium, 739 mg potassium

Rosemary Chicken

Make cleanup easy by marinating the chicken in a large plastic bag. After adding the marinade to the bag, place the bag in the baking dish. Then simply remove the chicken from the bag, and throw the bag and remaining marinade away.

4 medium skinless, boneless chicken breast halves (1 pound)

Marinade:
- ¼ **cup olive oil**
- 1 **tablespoon white wine vinegar**
- 1 **clove garlic, minced**
- ½ **teaspoon snipped fresh rosemary or** ¼ **teaspoon dried rosemary, crushed**
- ⅛ **teaspoon salt**
- ⅛ **teaspoon pepper**

Rinse the chicken in cold water; pat dry with paper towels. Place the chicken breasts in a baking dish.

Marinade: In a small bowl combine olive oil, vinegar, garlic, rosemary, salt, and pepper, mixing well. Pour marinade over the chicken. Cover and marinate in the refrigerator for 1 hour, turning once. Remove the chicken from the marinade; discard marinade.

Grill chicken in an uncovered grill directly over medium coals for 6 to 7 minutes on each side or until the chicken is tender and no pink remains.

Serves 4

Per serving: 232 calories, 20 g protein, 1 g carbohydrate, 16 g total fat (3 g saturated), 54 mg cholesterol, 117 mg sodium, 164 mg potassium

Grilled Chicken Tacos

To warm the tortillas, wrap them in foil and heat them in a 350° oven for about 10 minutes. Or, place them in a plastic bag and microwave them on 100% power (high) for about 30 seconds or until they are warm.

4 medium skinless, boneless chicken breast halves (1 pound)

Marinade:
2 tablespoons lime juice
2 tablespoons cooking oil
2 cloves garlic, minced
½ teaspoon chili powder
½ teaspoon ground cumin
¼ teaspoon dried oregano, crushed
¼ teaspoon crushed red pepper
¼ teaspoon salt
⅛ teaspoon black pepper

•••

4 10-inch flour tortillas, warmed

Toppings:
1 large tomato, chopped
1 avocado, seeded, peeled, and sliced
1 red onion, thinly sliced
½ cup shredded cheddar cheese (2 ounces)
Shredded lettuce
Salsa
Sour cream

Rinse the chicken breasts in cold water; pat dry with paper towels. Arrange chicken in a shallow baking dish.

Marinade: In a small bowl, combine lime juice, cooking oil, garlic, chili powder, cumin, oregano, crushed red pepper, salt, and black pepper. Mix well and pour over the chicken. Cover and marinate in the refrigerator for 1 hour, turning once. Remove the chicken from the marinade; discard marinade.

Grill the chicken in an uncovered grill over medium-hot coals for 12 to 15 minutes or until tender and no pink remains, turning once. Slice the chicken breasts crosswise into ½-inch strips.

To serve, place the chicken strips and toppings on half of each tortilla. Fold the other half of the tortilla over the chicken and toppings.

Serves 4

Per serving: 600 calories, 38 g protein, 45 g carbohydrate, 30 g total fat (10 g saturated), 10 mg cholesterol, 808 mg sodium, 898 mg potassium

Curried Kabobs

In this full-flavored meal, chunks of chicken are marinated in a mixture of yogurt and spices, then served with hot rice and a cool, crisp salad. The salad dressing is added to both the greens and chicken.

4 medium skinless, boneless chicken
    breast halves (12 ounces)

Marinade:

½ cup plain yogurt
2 cloves garlic, minced
½ teaspoon curry powder
½ teaspoon ground ginger
½ teaspoon chili powder
½ teaspoon salt
¼ teaspoon ground red pepper

Lemon Cilantro Dressing:

3 tablespoons lemon juice
2 tablespoons chopped cilantro
3 cloves garlic, minced
⅛ teaspoon salt
⅓ cup olive oil

•••

1 small head leaf lettuce, torn into
    pieces (6 cups)
1 large tomato, chopped
2 green onions, chopped

•••

2 or 3 cups cooked basmati or other
    long grain rice
    Fresh cilantro

Rinse the chicken in cold water; pat dry with paper towels. Cut the chicken into 1-inch pieces, and place the pieces in a large bowl.

Marinade: In a small bowl, combine the yogurt, garlic, curry powder, ginger, chili powder, salt, and red pepper. Pour over the chicken, and turn chicken pieces to coat. Cover and marinate in the refrigerator for 4 to 24 hours. Remove the chicken from the marinade; discard marinade.

Lemon Cilantro Dressing: In a small bowl, combine the lemon juice, cilantro, garlic, and salt. Whisk in the olive oil.

Thread the chicken pieces onto skewers. Grill them directly over medium-hot coals for 8 to 12 minutes or until chicken is tender and no pink remains, turning occasionally. Remove the chicken from skewers.

Meanwhile, in a large bowl, combine the lettuce, tomato, and green onions. Toss with half of the Lemon Cilantro Dressing.

Serve the chicken over the hot cooked rice with the salad. Spoon the remaining dressing over the chicken and rice. Garnish with fresh cilantro.

Serves 4 to 6

Per serving: 443 calories, 25 g protein, 37 g carbohydrate, 22 g total fat (4 g saturated), 55 mg cholesterol, 273 mg sodium, 573 mg potassium

Grilled Lemon Chicken

In this recipe, a whole chicken is grilled to a beautiful golden brown with crisp skin and moist meat. It's a snap to prepare.

1 2½- to 3-pound broiler-fryer chicken
2 small lemons
½ teaspoon salt
½ teaspoon pepper

Remove the giblets from the cavity of the chicken. Rinse the chicken in cold water; pat dry with paper towels.

With a fork, puncture the lemons on all sides. Sprinkle salt and pepper in the chicken's body cavity; add the lemons. Skewer neck skin to back; twist wings under back.

In a covered grill, arrange medium-hot coals around a drip pan; test for medium heat over drip pan. Place the chicken, breast side up, on the grill rack over the drip pan. Cover and grill for about 1 hour or until the drumsticks move easily in their sockets and the juices run clear.

To serve, remove the lemons, and cut the chicken into quarters.

Serves 4

Per serving: 342 calories, 39 g protein, 1 g carbohydrate, 19 g total fat (5 g saturated), 125 mg cholesterol, 383 mg sodium, 329 mg potassium

Turkey Breast with Maple Sauce

Break tradition this holiday season by grilling a turkey breast. The sauce, made with Vermont maple syrup, is especially tasty. Maple-flavored syrup also will yield a full maple flavor.

Maple Sauce:

- 1 tablespoon butter or margarine
- ¼ cup maple syrup
- 2 tablespoons brandy
- 1 gingersnap cookie, crushed
- 2 tablespoons chopped pecans

• • •

- 1 turkey breast half (about 2½ pounds)

Maple Sauce: Melt the butter or margarine in a small saucepan over medium heat. Add the maple syrup and brandy. Bring to boiling; boil gently for 1 minute. Add the crushed gingersnap a little at a time, stirring constantly until sauce thickens slightly. Stir in pecans; set aside.

Rinse the turkey breast in cold water; pat dry with paper towels.

In a covered grill, arrange medium-hot coals around the edges of the grill; test for medium heat over the center of the grill. Place the turkey breast on a rack in a roasting pan. Place in the center of the grill rack. Cover and grill for 1½ to 2 hours or until a thermometer registers 170°. (Add coals every 20 to 30 minutes, or as necessary, to maintain heat.) Brush turkey breast with sauce several times during the last 15 minutes of grilling. Remove turkey breast from grill; cover and let stand for 15 minutes before slicing.

Serves 6 to 8

Per serving: 289 calories, 30 g protein, 10 g carbohydrate, 12 g total fat (4 g saturated), 84 mg cholesterol, 92 mg sodium, 340 mg potassium

Chicken Salad with Oriental Flavors

Enjoy a meal of grilled chicken brushed with a soy-spice mixture, then served on a bed of spinach and drizzled with a soy vinaigrette.

Soy Vinaigrette:

⅓ cup red wine vinegar
1 tablespoon soy sauce
3 cloves garlic, minced
½ cup olive oil

•••

9 cups torn fresh spinach
1 11-ounce can mandarin orange
    sections, drained
1 large red onion, thinly sliced

•••

6 medium skinless, boneless chicken
    breast halves (about 1½ pounds)

•••

¼ cup soy sauce
1 tablespoon cooking oil
1 tablespoon honey
1 teaspoon five-spice powder
2 cloves garlic, minced
¼ teaspoon ground ginger

•••

2 avocados, peeled and sliced

Soy Vinaigrette: In a small bowl, combine the red wine vinegar, soy sauce, and garlic. Whisk in the olive oil. Set aside.

In a large bowl, combine the spinach, oranges, and onion; toss to mix.

Rinse the chicken in cold water; pat dry with paper towels.

In a small bowl, combine the soy sauce, oil, honey, five-spice powder, garlic, and ginger. Brush the chicken with the soy-spice mixture.

Grill the chicken in an uncovered grill directly over medium coals for 6 to 7 minutes. Turn and brush with the soy-spice mixture and cook for 6 to 7 minutes more.

Divide the spinach mixture among 6 individual plates. Slice each chicken breast into ½-inch slices. Place the chicken on the spinach. Arrange the avocado slices around the chicken. Drizzle each salad with some of the vinaigrette.

Serves 6

Per serving: 478 calories, 27 g protein, 20 g carbohydrate, 34 g total fat (5 g saturated), 60 mg cholesterol, 989 mg sodium, 1,185 mg potassium

Moroccan Flank Steak

Marinate flank steak in an exotic combination of Moroccan spices and quickly grill it over medium coals. Slice the meat into thin strips and serve with plain couscous or Orange-Cumin Couscous (page 147).

2 pounds flank steak, ¾ to 1 inch thick

Marinade:
- ⅓ **cup olive oil**
- 2 **tablespoons snipped fresh parsley**
- 2 **tablespoons lemon juice**
- 1½ **teaspoons chili powder**
- 1½ **teaspoons ground cumin**
- 1 **teaspoon ground coriander**
- 1 **teaspoon ground ginger**
- 1 **teaspoon soy sauce**
- 2 **cloves garlic, minced**
- ½ **teaspoon ground cinnamon**
- ½ **teaspoon dried oregano, crushed**
- ½ **teaspoon salt**
- ¼ **teaspoon black pepper**
- ¼ to ½ **teaspoon ground red pepper**

•••

Hot cooked couscous

Trim the steak of excess fat. Place steak in a large, shallow baking dish.

Marinade: In a small bowl, combine olive oil, parsley, lemon juice, chili powder, cumin, coriander, ginger, soy sauce, garlic, cinnamon, oregano, salt, black pepper, and red pepper. Pour over the steak; turn to coat. Cover and marinate in the refrigerator for 4 to 6 hours. Turn steak once or twice while marinating. Remove the steak from the marinade; discard marinade.

Grill steak directly over medium coals for 12 to 14 minutes, turning once, for medium doneness. Let stand for 5 minutes before cutting into ½-inch slices. Serve with hot cooked couscous.

Serves 8

Per serving: 345 calories, 25 g protein, 23 g carbohydrate, 17 g total fat (5 g saturated), 53 mg cholesterol, 252 mg sodium, 507 mg potassium

Flank Steak Salad with Cumin Vinaigrette

This is the perfect "salad dinner" to serve in your own backyard on a hot summer evening. It is hearty enough for meat lovers but has a contemporary lightness.

1 1 to 1¼ pound flank steak

Marinade:
½ cup olive oil
2 tablespoons red wine vinegar
1 teaspoon salt
½ teaspoon Dijon-style mustard
1 clove garlic, minced
¼ teaspoon black pepper
¼ teaspoon crushed red pepper

•••

1 small ripe avocado, pitted, peeled, and sliced
1 small red onion, thinly sliced

Cumin Vinaigrette:
2 tablespoons red wine vinegar
1 clove garlic, minced
¼ teaspoon ground cumin
⅛ teaspoon black pepper
Dash salt
3 tablespoons olive oil

•••

1 head Boston leaf lettuce or other leaf lettuce
1 medium tomato, cut into wedges

Trim excess fat from steak. Rinse steak; pat dry with paper towels.

Marinade: In a small bowl, combine olive oil, red wine vinegar, salt, mustard, garlic, black pepper, and crushed red pepper. Pour ¼ cup of the marinade over the steak, turning to coat both sides. Set remaining marinade aside. Cover steak and marinate in the refrigerator for 1 to 24 hours, turning steak occasionally. Remove the steak from the marinade; discard marinade.

About 30 minutes before serving, place the sliced avocado and onion in a bowl; pour the remaining marinade over the top. Toss to coat; cover and refrigerate.

Grill the steak directly over medium coals for 12 to 14 minutes for medium doneness, turning once. Remove the steak from the grill, and let it stand for 5 minutes before slicing.

Cumin Vinaigrette: In a small bowl, combine red wine vinegar, garlic, cumin, black pepper, and salt. Whisk in the olive oil.

Slice the flank steak into thin slices. Line a large platter with lettuce leaves. Arrange the steak, avocado, onion, and tomato on the platter. Stir the vinaigrette, and spoon it evenly over the steak. Pass the remaining vinaigrette.

Serves 4 to 6

Per serving: 603 calories, 26 g protein, 11 g carbohydrate, 52 g total fat (10 g saturated), 57 mg cholesterol, 674 mg sodium, 930 mg potassium

Ragin' Cajun Rib Eyes

The hearty rib eye is the steak of choice for this tangy mix. Just rub the steaks with the spice mixture and grill over medium coals. Unlike steak sauces, the rub bolsters the rib eye's flavor without masking its unmatched taste.

2 8 ounce beef rib eye steaks, cut
   ¾ inch thick
2 cloves garlic, minced

Spice Mixture:

1 teaspoon coarsely ground black
   pepper
½ teaspoon onion powder
½ teaspoon dried thyme, crushed
½ teaspoon dried oregano, crushed
½ teaspoon paprika
½ teaspoon crushed red pepper
¼ teaspoon salt

Rub equal amounts of minced garlic into both sides of the steaks.

Spice Mixture: In a small bowl, combine black pepper, onion powder, thyme, oregano, paprika, crushed red pepper, and salt. Rub equal amounts into both sides of the steaks.

Grill the steaks directly over medium heat for 8 to 12 minutes (rare) or 12 to 15 minutes (medium), turning meat over halfway through grilling. To serve, cut each steak in half.

Serves 4

Per serving: 213 calories, 24 g protein, 1 g carbohydrate, 12 g total fat (5 g saturated), 68 mg cholesterol, 195 mg sodium, 347 mg potassium

Filets with Sauce Bordelaise

Sauce Bordelaise, a traditional bond of wine, broth, and herbs, is the perfect complement to beef tenderloin filets. To make this meal a French classic, serve them with Potatoes Parisian (page 140), crusty French Bread (page 182), and a green vegetable. Offer a full-bodied red wine, and follow the main course with a crisp green salad.

4 beef tenderloin filets, cut 1 inch thick
    (1 to 1¼ pounds total)
Salt

Sauce Bordelaise:

1 cup dry red wine
2 green onions, chopped
¼ teaspoon dried marjoram, crushed, or
    ¾ teaspoon snipped fresh marjoram
¼ teaspoon dried thyme, crushed, or
    ¾ teaspoon snipped fresh thyme
⅛ teaspoon pepper
1 small bay leaf
1 cup beef broth
2 teaspoons cornstarch
2 tablespoons beef broth or water
1 teaspoon lemon juice
1 tablespoon butter or margarine

Grill the filets directly over medium coals for 4 to 6 minutes. Turn the filets over and sprinkle with salt. Grill for 4 to 6 minutes more for medium-rare doneness. (Or, grill 6 to 8 minutes per side for medium doneness.)

Sauce Bordelaise: In a large skillet, combine the red wine, green onions, marjoram, thyme, pepper, and bay leaf. Bring to boiling; reduce heat. Simmer, uncovered, until mixture is reduced by half. Add the 1 cup beef broth, and simmer until mixture is reduced by half. Strain the sauce through a fine sieve, and return it to the skillet. Combine the cornstarch and 2 tablespoons of beef broth or water. Add it to the sauce slowly, stirring until the sauce bubbles and thickens slightly. Cook 2 minutes more. Remove from heat, and stir in lemon juice and butter or margarine. Serve over filets.

Serves 4

Per serving: 259 calories, 25 g protein, 3 g carbohydrate, 12 g total fat (5 g saturated), 79 mg cholesterol, 307 mg sodium, 472 mg potassium

Adobo Pork Chops

Adobo refers to a variety of vinegar-based, red chili sauces. In this recipe, lime juice, rather than vinegar, brightens the flavor of the adobo used to marinate the pork chops before grilling.

4 boneless pork loin chops, cut 1 inch thick

Marinade:

1 8-ounce can tomato sauce
¼ cup finely chopped onion
2 tablespoons lime juice
1 tablespoon cooking oil
1 teaspoon chili powder
1 teaspoon ground cumin
2 cloves garlic, minced
½ teaspoon salt
¼ teaspoon dried oregano, crushed
¼ teaspoon crushed red pepper
¼ teaspoon black pepper

Trim the excess fat from the pork chops, and place them in a shallow baking dish.

Marinade: In a small bowl, combine the tomato sauce, onion, lime juice, cooking oil, chili powder, cumin, garlic, salt, oregano, crushed red pepper, and black pepper. Pour the marinade over the pork chops and turn to coat. Cover and marinate in the refrigerator for 2 to 24 hours.

Grill chops, thickly coated with the marinade, directly over medium coals for about 20 to 25 minutes or until juices run clear, turning once and basting with remaining marinade. (Do not baste during the last 10 minutes of grilling.)

Serves 4

Per serving: 332 calories, 32 g protein, 7 g carbohydrate, 20 g total fat (6 g saturated), 103 mg cholesterol, 696 mg sodium, 683 mg potassium

Sesame Pork Kabobs

These full-flavored kabobs are accompanied by a noodle and vegetable combination that you can cook while the grill heats.

1¼ to 1½ pounds whole pork tenderloin

Marinade:
¼ cup soy sauce
1 tablespoon dry white wine
2 teaspoons honey
1 teaspoon cooking oil
1 clove garlic, minced
½ teaspoon grated fresh gingerroot
¼ teaspoon five-spice powder

•••

2 teaspoons sesame seeds

•••

8 ounces medium egg noodles
½ teaspoon roasted sesame oil
1 tablespoon cooking oil
6 green onions, diagonally sliced into
    1-inch pieces
1 teaspoon grated fresh gingerroot
1 medium red sweet pepper, cut into
    thin strips
8 ounces Chinese cabbage, thinly sliced
    (2 cups)
3 tablespoons soy sauce

Trim the excess fat from the pork tenderloin, and slice it into 1-inch pieces. Place pork slices in a shallow baking dish.

Marinade: In a medium bowl, combine the soy sauce, wine, honey, oil, garlic, gingerroot, and five-spice powder. Place the pork in the marinade and turn to coat. Cover and marinate in the refrigerator for 2 hours, turning occasionally.

Remove meat from marinade, reserving marinade. Divide the meat among 4 to 6 metal skewers. Sprinkle with the sesame seeds. Cover and chill until needed.

Cook the egg noodles according to package directions; drain and set aside. Heat a wok or large skillet over medium-high heat; add the sesame oil and cooking oil. (Add more cooking oil as necessary during cooking.) Add the green onions, gingerroot, red pepper, and cabbage; stir-fry for 2 minutes. Add the cooked noodles and stir-fry for 2 minutes. Add the 3 tablespoons soy sauce and stir-fry for 1 minute more. Cover and keep warm while grilling kabobs.

Grill kabobs directly over medium coals for 12 to 14 minutes, turning and brushing once or twice with remaining marinade during the first 8 minutes of grilling.

Serve the kabobs with the noodle-vegetable mixture.

Serves 6

Per serving: 334 calories, 28 g protein, 33 g carbohydrate, 10 g total fat (2 g saturated), 126 mg cholesterol, 1289 mg sodium, 678 mg potassium

Grilled Pork Chops with Soy Vinaigrette

Choose either a bone-in pork loin chop or rib chop for this subtly flavored, marinated meat.

**4 pork loin chops, cut 1 inch thick
(about 2 pounds total)**

Soy-Vinaigrette Marinade:
¼ **cup olive oil**
2 **tablespoons soy sauce**
1 **tablespoon red wine vinegar**
1½ **teaspoons roasted sesame oil**
2 **cloves garlic, minced**
½ **teaspoon crushed red pepper**

Trim excess fat from pork chops. Place the pork chops in a shallow baking dish.

Soy-Vinaigrette Marinade: In a small bowl, combine olive oil, soy sauce, red wine vinegar, sesame oil, garlic, and crushed red pepper. Pour the marinade over the pork chops. Cover and marinate in the refrigerator for 2 hours. Remove the pork chops from the marinade; discard marinade.

Grill the chops directly over medium coals for 10 to 12 minutes on each side or until the meat near the bone is no longer pink.

Serves 4

Per serving: 221 calories, 27 g protein, 1 g carbohydrate, 12 g total fat (3 g saturated), 68 mg cholesterol, 228 mg sodium, 369 mg potassium

Grilled Pork Tenderloin Salad

To easily cut up fresh herbs, place the leaves in a small glass measuring cup and use kitchen scissors to snip them into small pieces. Or, if you prefer, the leaves may be finely chopped with a chef's knife.

2 12-ounce whole pork tenderloins

Marinade:
3 tablespoons olive oil
3 cloves garlic, minced
1 tablespoon snipped fresh parsley
1 teaspoon snipped fresh lemon thyme or thyme
1 teaspoon snipped fresh rosemary
¼ teaspoon salt
¼ teaspoon pepper

• • •

¾ cup apple wood smoking chips

Balsamic Vinaigrette:
⅓ cup olive oil
2 tablespoons balsamic vinegar
3 cloves garlic, minced
⅛ teaspoon salt

• • •

10 cups torn Boston leaf lettuce or torn mixed greens
2 orange, red, or green sweet peppers, thinly sliced
2 tomatoes, sliced

Trim excess fat from the tenderloin. To butterfly each tenderloin, make a long, shallow slit along the length of the meat, and gently press it open. Make another slit on each side of the first slit, and press the meat flat. (Do not cut completely through the meat.) Place the meat in a large shallow baking dish.

Marinade: In a small bowl, combine the olive oil, garlic, parsley, lemon thyme or thyme, rosemary, salt, and pepper. Brush the mixture generously over the meat. Cover and marinate in the refrigerator for 1 to 24 hours.

Place the apple wood chips on a 12x10-inch piece of aluminum foil, and seal tightly to make a foil packet. Pierce the foil in several places to allow the smoke to escape.

In a covered grill, arrange medium-hot coals around a drip pan; test for medium heat over the pan. Place the foil packet of chips on coals. Place the tenderloins on the grill rack over the drip pan. Cover and grill for 20 to 25 minutes or until the juices run clear. Slice the pork crosswise into ¼-inch slices.

Balsamic Vinaigrette: In a small jar that has a lid, combine the oil, vinegar, garlic, and salt. Cover and shake well.

To serve, divide the lettuce among 6 individual plates. Arrange the sliced pork, sweet peppers, and tomatoes on the lettuce. Drizzle with the vinaigrette.

Serves 6

Per serving: 339 calories, 27 g protein, 7 g carbohydrate, 23 g total fat (4 g saturated), 79 mg cholesterol, 202 mg sodium, 853 mg potassium

Pork Tenderloin Americana

Pork tenderloin goes all-American stuffed with corn bread, herbs, and walnuts and wrapped with bacon. Grill and slice into rounds for an attractive presentation. To oven-roast the pork, place the tenderloins on a rack in a shallow baking pan. Bake in a 350° oven for 40 to 45 minutes or until the juices run clear. Brush meat with the pan drippings after 30 minutes.

2 whole pork tenderloins (about
    1½ pounds total)

Onion Stuffing:

  6 tablespoons butter or margarine
  3 cups chopped onion
  3 cloves garlic, minced
1½ cups corn bread stuffing mix
  1 tablespoon snipped fresh parsley
  1 teaspoon snipped fresh thyme or
    ¼ teaspoon dried thyme, crushed
  1 teaspoon snipped fresh sage or
    ¼ teaspoon dried sage, crushed
  4 to 6 tablespoons chicken broth
¼ cup walnuts, chopped

     •••

  4 strips bacon
  4 teaspoons coarsely ground pepper

Trim excess fat from tenderloins. Cut a long, shallow slit along the length of each tenderloin, and gently press it open. (Do not cut completely through the meat.) Place each tenderloin between 2 sheets of plastic wrap. Use the flat side of a meat mallet to pound the meat to about ⅜-inch thickness.

Onion Stuffing: Melt the butter or margarine in a saucepan over medium-low heat. Add the onion and garlic and cook until the onion is tender. Remove the pan from the heat, and add the stuffing mix, parsley, thyme, and sage. Add enough of the chicken broth to moisten the mixture, mixing well. Stir in the walnuts.

Spread half of the stuffing on each tenderloin, and roll up. Criss-cross two strips of bacon, and wrap bacon strips around each tenderloin. Secure with toothpicks. Rub 2 teaspoons of the pepper into each tenderloin.

In a covered grill, arrange medium-hot coals around a drip pan; test for medium heat over the drip pan. Place the tenderloins on the grill rack over the drip pan. Cover and grill for 45 minutes or until the juices run clear. Remove tenderloins from the grill. Remove toothpicks and cut into ¾-inch slices.

Serves 6

Per serving: 445 calories, 31 g protein, 30 g carbohydrate, 22 g total fat (10 g saturated), 114 mg cholesterol, 649 mg sodium, 722 mg potassium

Grilled Pork with Pita Bread

Serve this for a casual meal when friends are dining with you. Set out the bread and all of the toppings and let your guests make their own sandwiches. You can easily double the recipe for a larger crowd.

1 1-pound whole pork tenderloin

Spice Rub:
¼ teaspoon dried oregano, crushed
¼ teaspoon dried marjoram, crushed
¼ teaspoon dried thyme, crushed
¼ teaspoon salt
¼ teaspoon pepper

•••

2 tablespoons olive oil
2 cloves garlic, minced

•••

6 pita bread rounds

Toppings:
Plain yogurt
Shredded spinach leaves
6 yellow or red cherry tomatoes,
   cut into wedges
½ of a medium red onion, sliced
Crumbled feta cheese
Roasted red sweet pepper strips

Trim excess fat from the pork tenderloin. To butterfly the tenderloin, make a long, shallow slit along the length of the meat, and gently press it open. Make another slit on each side of the first slit, and press the meat flat. (Do not cut completely through the meat.)

Spice Rub: In a small bowl combine oregano, marjoram, thyme, salt, and pepper. Rub the mixture into both sides of the tenderloin.

Place the meat in a shallow baking pan. Combine the olive oil and garlic. Brush the meat generously with the oil mixture. Cover and refrigerate for 1 to 24 hours.

Grill the pork tenderloin over medium heat for 6 to 7 minutes on each side or until the juices run clear. Slice the meat into thin strips, and serve with pita bread and toppings of yogurt, shredded spinach, tomato wedges, onion slices, crumbled cheese, and pepper strips.

Serves 6

Per serving: 359 calories, 26 g protein, 40 g carbohydrate, 11 g total fat (3 g saturated), 63 mg cholesterol, 589 mg sodium, 617 mg potassium

Smoked Scallops with Mustard Marmalade

Wild rice is the perfect side dish for these delicately flavored scallops. The marmalade is equally good served over fish filets.

1 pound sea scallops
¼ cup butter or margarine, melted

Mustard Marmalade:

⅓ cup orange marmalade
1 tablespoon coarse-grain mustard
1½ teaspoons soy sauce

•••

½ cup apple wood smoking chips

Rinse scallops in cold water and drain well. Thread scallops onto metal or wooden skewers. (If using wooden skewers, soak them in water for 1 hour before using.) Brush with some of the melted butter or margarine.

Mustard Marmalade: In a small saucepan, combine orange marmalade, mustard, and soy sauce. Cook and stir over low heat until heated through.

Place the apple wood chips on a 12x10-inch piece of aluminum foil, and seal tightly to make a foil packet. Pierce the foil in several places to allow the smoke to escape.

Arrange medium-hot coals around a drip pan; test for medium heat over the drip pan. Place foil packet on coals, and wait for chips to begin smoking. Place the scallops on the grill rack over the drip pan. Grill for 5 to 7 minutes or until opaque, brushing with remaining melted butter or margarine once.

To serve, divide Mustard Marmalade among 4 individual plates; add the scallops.

Serves 4

Per serving: 313 calories, 21 g protein, 23 g carbohydrate, 16 g total fat (8 g saturated), 71 mg cholesterol, 822 mg sodium, 414 mg potassium

Scallops on Pasta with Spinach

If the weather doesn't permit grilling, broil the scallops 4 to 5 inches from the heat for 8 to 10 minutes or until they are opaque.

1 pound sea scallops
1 tablespoon olive oil
⅓ cup fine dry bread crumbs
¼ teaspoon salt

• • •

8 ounces angel hair pasta
4 cups fresh spinach, sliced into ½-inch
    strips

• • •

¼ cup pine nuts
2 tablespoons oil from oil-pack dried
    tomatoes or olive oil
3 green onions, thinly sliced (⅓ cup)
2 cloves garlic, minced
½ cup dried tomatoes in oil, drained and
    sliced into thin strips

• • •

½ cup crumbled feta cheese

Rinse the scallops in cold water and drain well. Thread them onto metal skewers, and brush them with olive oil. Combine the bread crumbs and salt; sprinkle over the scallops.

Grill the scallops directly over medium coals for 5 to 8 minutes or until opaque, turning the skewers often. Keep warm until ready to serve.

Meanwhile, cook pasta according to package directions. Place spinach in a large colander. Drain pasta by pouring it over the spinach. Return pasta and spinach to hot pan.

In a medium skillet, cook pine nuts in the oil from the tomatoes or olive oil until they just begin to brown. Add green onion and garlic; cook until onion is tender. Add onion mixture and tomatoes to pasta and spinach; toss to coat.

Divide pasta mixture among 4 individual plates. Arrange the scallops on the pasta and sprinkle with feta cheese.

Serves 4

Per serving: 632 calories, 34 g protein, 62 g carbohydrate, 30 g total fat (7 g saturated), 61 mg cholesterol, 1,084 mg sodium, 1,153 mg potassium

Curried Fish Kabobs

Present these spicy fish kabobs on top of a wild-and-white-rice combination. Another time, try the marinade with chicken.

1½ pounds halibut steaks, cut
　　1½ inches thick

Marinade:

　1　8-ounce carton plain yogurt
　3　cloves garlic, minced
　½　teaspoon salt
　½　teaspoon curry powder
　½　teaspoon chili powder
　½　teaspoon ground ginger

　　　•••

　1　green sweet pepper
　1　red sweet pepper
　1　yellow or orange sweet pepper
　½　of a medium pineapple

Cut the fish into 1½-inch pieces; discard skin and bones.

Marinade: In a large bowl, combine yogurt, garlic, salt, curry powder, chili powder, and ginger. Place the fish in the marinade and turn gently to coat. Cover and marinate in the refrigerator for 2 hours. Remove fish pieces from the marinade; discard marinade.

Meanwhile, cut the peppers into 1½-inch pieces. Cut pineapple into wedges or spears. Thread the fish pieces onto metal skewers, alternating with the pepper pieces and pineapple chunks.

Grill the kabobs directly over medium coals for 12 to 18 minutes or until the fish flakes easily, turning once.

Serves 4

Per serving: 258 calories, 37 g protein, 16 g carbohydrate, 5 g total fat (1 g saturated), 55 mg cholesterol, 298 mg sodium, 1,068 mg potassium

Grilled Lamb Chops

One of the simplest ways to enjoy lamb chops is to grill them. Just marinate the chops for a few hours in a red wine vinaigrette with mustard, garlic, and tarragon, then cook quickly over hot coals. Serve with New Potatoes with Rosemary (page 139).

8 lamb loin or rib chops, cut ¾ inch thick (about 1½ pounds total)

Marinade:
2 tablespoons red wine vinegar
1 teaspoon Dijon-style mustard
2 cloves garlic, minced
1 teaspoon snipped fresh tarragon or
⅛ teaspoon dried tarragon, crushed
⅛ teaspoon salt
⅛ teaspoon pepper
¼ cup olive oil

Trim the fat from the lamb chops, and place them in a shallow baking dish.

Marinade: In a small bowl, combine the red wine vinegar, mustard, garlic, tarragon, salt, and pepper. Whisk in the olive oil. Pour over the chops and turn to coat. Cover and marinate in the refrigerator for 4 to 6 hours, turning chops occasionally. Remove the lamb chops from the marinade; discard marinade.

Grill the chops in an uncovered grill directly over medium-hot coals for 10 to 14 minutes for medium doneness or until the desired doneness is achieved, turning once.

Serves 4

Per serving: 262 calories, 28 g protein, 1 g carbohydrate, 16 g total fat (4 g saturated), 87 mg cholesterol, 130 mg sodium, 353 mg potassium

Grilled Mushrooms

Grilled button mushrooms make a great appetizer. They also are a delicious side dish for grilled meats.

1 pound fresh button mushrooms,
    rinsed

•••

2 teaspoons snipped fresh marjoram or
    ½ teaspoon dried marjoram,
    crushed
2 teaspoons snipped fresh marjoram or
    ½ teaspoon dried thyme, crushed
1 teaspoon onion powder
1 teaspoon garlic powder
¼ cup butter or margarine, cut into
    chunks

Rinse the mushrooms; pat dry with paper towels. Place them on an 18x18-inch piece of heavy duty aluminum foil. Sprinkle the mushrooms with marjoram, thyme, onion powder, and garlic powder. Top them with chunks of butter or margarine. Close the foil over the mushrooms, leaving the top open slightly.

In a covered grill, arrange medium-hot coals around a drip pan; test for medium heat over the drip pan. Place foil pouch on the grill rack over the drip pan; cover grill. Grill for about 30 minutes or until mushrooms are tender.

Serves 4

Per serving: 135 calories, 3 g protein, 6 g carbohydrate, 12 g total fat (7 g saturated), 31 mg cholesterol, 122 mg sodium, 437 mg potassium

Grilled Sweet Onions

More than just a flavor enhancer, this savory grilled vegetable takes its rightful place on the plate, equal to any vegetable accompaniment. For a different flavor combination, omit the bacon and add 2 tablespoons butter or margarine to the foil pouch along with a sprig of fresh dill or thyme.

4 small sweet yellow onions
  (about 5 to 6 ounces each)
4 bacon strips
  Salt
  Pepper

Peel onions. Cut an X three-quarters of the way through each onion.

Place each onion on a 12x12-inch piece of aluminum foil. Cut the bacon strips in half crosswise, and cross them over the tops of the onions. Sprinkle with salt and pepper. Fold the foil securely around each onion and seal tightly.

In a covered grill, arrange medium-hot coals around a drip pan; test for medium heat above the drip pan. Place the onions on the grill rack over the drip pan. Cover and grill for 45 to 60 minutes or until the onions are tender and juices begin to caramelize.

Serves 4

Per serving: 216 calories, 4 g protein, 12 g carbohydrate, 17 g total fat (8 g saturated), 20 mg cholesterol, 315 mg sodium, 255 mg potassium

Pouch Potatoes

A little change in serving style will make the traditional potato the center of attention. Serve with grilled steaks or chicken. If you have a food processor, slice the onion with a thin blade.

4 medium baking potatoes
2 medium onions, very thinly sliced
3 to 4 tablespoons butter or margarine
Salt
Pepper

Wash the potatoes. Cut very thin slices in each potato, about ¾ of the way through, leaving the potato whole. Place each potato on a 7x7-inch piece of heavy duty aluminum foil.

Thinly slice the onions into rings. Insert the onion rings between the slices of the potato. Dot each potato with some of the butter or margarine. Generously salt and pepper each potato and wrap tightly in the foil.

Place the potatoes on the grill rack directly over medium-slow coals. Cover and grill for 1 to 2 hours or until the potatoes are tender.

Serves 4

Per serving: 318 calories, 5 g protein, 56 g carbohydrate, 9 g total fat (5 g saturated), 23 mg cholesterol, 239 mg sodium, 939 mg potassium

Pasta Prima

Colorful, tempting pasta dishes delight nearly everyone's palate. Take a chance on something new with one of our robust main dishes or quick side dishes.

Fettuccine with Broccoli and Garlic

Tender, crisp broccoli makes a colorful topping for pasta. Chopped garlic cooked to a golden brown, crushed red pepper, and Parmesan cheese broaden the flavor of this colorful side dish.

12 ounces broccoli
2 tablespoons olive oil
4 cloves garlic, finely chopped
⅛ teaspoon crushed red pepper
    Salt

•••

8 ounces dried red pepper fettuccine or
    plain fettuccine, cooked and
    drained
    Finely shredded Parmesan cheese

Chop the broccoli flowerets into bite-size pieces. Peel the stalk and chop it into bite-size pieces. (You should have 4 cups of broccoli pieces.) Cook the broccoli, covered, in a small amount of boiling water for about 5 minutes or until crisp-tender; drain well.

Heat the olive oil in a large skillet over medium heat. Add the garlic and stir gently until garlic begins to turn golden (2 to 3 minutes). Watch closely to make sure the garlic doesn't burn. Add the crushed red pepper and the cooked broccoli. Cook and stir for 1 minute. Sprinkle with salt to taste. Toss the broccoli mixture with the hot cooked fettuccine. Sprinkle with Parmesan cheese.

Makes 6 side-dish servings

Per serving: 228 calories, 9 g protein, 32 g carbohydrate, 7 g total fat (2 g saturated), 13 mg cholesterol, 223 mg sodium, 273 mg potassium

Fettuccine with Artichoke Sauce

This delicate pasta dish, with a sauce of artichoke hearts, tomatoes, and cream, makes a soft, pastel presentation. Serve it as a meatless entrée or as a side dish with grilled Italian sausages. Because it's a quick "one-pan" dish, it's a great choice for easy entertaining.

2 tablespoons olive oil
1 tablespoon butter or margarine
1 cup chopped onion
2 cloves garlic, finely chopped

•••

1 14½-ounce can Italian tomatoes, undrained and cut up
½ cup chicken broth
2 tablespoons snipped fresh basil or 2 teaspoons dried basil, crushed

•••

1 13¾-ounce can artichoke hearts, drained and chopped
1 cup whipping cream
¼ teaspoon salt
⅛ teaspoon white pepper

•••

8 ounces dried fettuccine, cooked and drained
¼ cup finely shredded Parmesan cheese
Nutmeg

Heat the olive oil and butter or margarine in a large skillet over medium heat. Add the onion and garlic, and cook until tender but not brown.

Stir in the undrained tomatoes, chicken broth, and basil. Bring to boiling; reduce heat. Simmer, uncovered, over medium-high heat for 8 to 10 minutes or until liquid is reduced by half.

Add the artichoke hearts, whipping cream, salt, and pepper. Simmer for 5 to 10 minutes more or until sauce thickens slightly.

Serve the artichoke sauce over the hot cooked fettuccine. Top with grated Parmesan cheese and sprinkle with nutmeg.

Makes 4 main-dish or 8 side-dish servings

Per serving: 597 calories, 14 g protein, 58 g carbohydrate, 35 g total fat (18 g saturated), 106 mg cholesterol, 623 mg sodium, 628 mg potassium

Spaghetti with Italian Sausage

This rich, smooth tomato sauce with Italian sausage can be prepared in just 40 minutes. Serve with a salad and garlic bread.
To significantly lower the sodium in the sauce, use canned tomato sauce with no salt added.

2 tablespoons butter or margarine
¼ cup finely chopped onion
2 cloves garlic, minced
2 15-ounce cans tomato sauce
2 teaspoons sugar
2 tablespoons snipped fresh basil or
    2 teaspoons dried basil, crushed
1 tablespoon snipped fresh oregano or
    1 teaspoon dried oregano, crushed
⅛ teaspoon pepper
3 to 4 links hot Italian sausage

•••

12 ounces dried spaghetti, cooked and
    drained
    Grated Parmesan cheese

Melt the butter or margarine in a large saucepan over low heat. Add the onion and garlic. Cook slowly, stirring occasionally, until the onion is tender. Add the tomato sauce, sugar, basil, oregano, and pepper. Simmer over low heat, partially covered (lid slightly ajar), for 20 minutes, stirring occasionally.

Meanwhile, remove the sausage from the casings, and cut it into 1-inch pieces. Brown in a skillet over medium heat, turning frequently. Remove with a slotted spoon and drain on paper towels. After the sauce has simmered for 20 minutes, add the sausage. Simmer, covered, for 20 minutes more, stirring occasionally.

Serve the sauce over hot cooked spaghetti with Parmesan cheese.

Makes 6 main-dish servings

Per serving: 492 calories, 21 g protein, 59 g carbohydrate, 19 g total fat (8 g saturated), 53 mg cholesterol, 1,411 mg sodium, 769 mg potassium

Spaghetti with Fresh Tomato Sauce

Take advantage of vine-ripened tomatoes to make your own fresh tomato sauce for pasta. It's easy and economical.

2 tablespoons olive oil
1 cup finely chopped onion
3 cloves garlic, minced

•••

4 cups peeled, chopped tomatoes
    (2½ pounds)
2 tablespoons snipped fresh basil or
    2 teaspoons dried basil, crushed
1½ teaspoons snipped fresh oregano or
    ½ teaspoon dried oregano, chopped
2 teaspoons sugar
½ teaspoon salt
¼ teaspoon crushed red pepper

•••

6 ounces dried spaghetti, cooked and
    drained
    Finely shredded Parmesan cheese

Heat the olive oil in a medium skillet over low heat. Add the onion and garlic and cook, stirring occasionally, until the onion is tender but not brown.

Add the tomatoes, basil, oregano, sugar, salt, and crushed red pepper. Bring to boiling; reduce heat. Simmer, uncovered, over medium heat, stirring occasionally, for 15 to 20 minutes or until most of the liquid has evaporated and the sauce thickens slightly. Taste and adjust seasonings, if necessary.

Serve sauce over hot cooked spaghetti with Parmesan cheese.

Makes 4 side-dish servings

Per serving: 311 calories, 10 g protein, 47 g carbohydrate, 10 g total fat (2 g saturated), 5 mg cholesterol, 403 mg sodium, 487 mg potassium

Gold Nugget Linguine

Combine this simple side dish with any broiled or grilled meat and your favorite vegetable for a quick meal.

¾ cup dry bread crumbs (about 3 slices white bread)

•••

8 ounces dried linguini
3 tablespoons butter or margarine

•••

2 tablespoons olive oil
3 cloves garlic, finely chopped
¼ cup grated Romano or Parmesan cheese
Pepper
2 tablespoons snipped fresh parsley

To make the bread crumbs, blend or process the bread in a blender or food processor until coarse, medium-fine crumbs are produced. Measure ¾ cup and set aside.

Cook linguine according to package directions; drain. Toss linguine with butter or margarine. Cover and keep warm.

Heat the olive oil in a large skillet over medium heat. Add the garlic and stir constantly for 30 seconds. Add the bread crumbs and cook, turning often with a spatula, until the crumbs are golden brown (about 5 minutes). Watch carefully to avoid burning the mixture.

Add the linguine. Turn gently to coat with the crumb mixture; heat through. Remove the skillet from the heat and add the Romano or Parmesan cheese. Add pepper to taste. Toss gently to combine. Sprinkle with parsley.

Makes 8 side-dish servings

Per serving: 195 calories, 6 g protein, 30 g carbohydrate, 5 g total fat (1 g saturated), 4 mg cholesterol, 113 mg sodium, 52 mg potassium

Radiatore and Cheese

Sharp cheddar cheese, tomato, green onion, and garlic add a jazzy taste to this version of macaroni and cheese.

12 ounces dried radiatore or corkscrew
    macaroni
1½ cups shredded sharp cheddar cheese
    (6 ounces)
1½ cups chopped fresh tomatoes
  2 green onions, chopped
  1 tablespoon snipped fresh oregano or
    ½ teaspoon dried oregano, crushed
  1 clove garlic, minced

        •••

  1 cup milk
  2 tablespoons all-purpose flour
  ½ teaspoon salt

Cook the radiatore or corkscrew macaroni according to package directions; drain well. Return pasta to the warm pan. Gently stir in the cheese, tomatoes, green onion, oregano, and garlic.

Pour the milk into a jar that has a lid. Add the flour and salt. Cover and shake well to combine. Stir the milk mixture into the radiatore mixture. Cook, stirring gently, over medium heat until the cheese has melted and the mixture is thick and bubbly (about 3 to 4 minutes).

Makes 5 or 6 main-dish servings

Per serving: 438 calories, 19 g protein, 59 g carbohydrate, 14 g total fat (8 g saturated), 54 mg cholesterol, 457 mg sodium, 364 mg potassium

Spinach Linguine with Sweet Onions

Onion and garlic, slowly cooked in butter and olive oil, gives this dish a savory sweetness. Chicken broth, wine, and herbs add a light finish to the sauce.

3 medium onions (1 pound)
1 tablespoon olive oil
1 tablespoon butter or margarine
2 cloves garlic, minced

• • •

⅓ cup chicken broth
⅓ cup dry white wine
1 tablespoon snipped fresh basil or
    1 teaspoon dried basil, crushed
1 teaspoon snipped fresh oregano or
    ¼ teaspoon dried oregano, crushed
¼ teaspoon pepper

• • •

8 ounces refrigerated spinach linguine,
    cooked and drained
¼ cup grated Parmesan cheese

Cut the onions in half lengthwise and remove skins. Place flat side down on a cutting board and slice thinly. (You should have 3 to 3½ cups sliced onions.)

Heat the olive oil and butter in a large saucepan or Dutch oven over medium-low heat. Add the onions and garlic and cover. Cook slowly, stirring occasionally, until the onions are very tender but not brown (about 30 minutes). Lower the heat if the onions begin to brown or stick to the pan.

Add the chicken broth, wine, basil, oregano, and pepper. Raise the heat to medium-high and simmer, uncovered, for 4 to 6 minutes, stirring occasionally, until the liquid is reduced by half. Add the hot cooked linguine and Parmesan cheese. Mix well and heat thoroughly.

Makes 4 side-dish servings

Per serving: 230 calories, 7 g protein, 28 g carbohydrate, 9 g total fat (4 g saturated), 13 mg cholesterol, 238 mg sodium, 248 mg potassium

Super Soups and Stews

Once you glance through this chapter, you'll realize not all soups and stews come in a can. In fact, old and sure-to-be new favorite recipes may just entice you to simmer a homemade soup or stew this weekend.

Mexican Corn Chowder

This hearty corn chowder is spiced with cumin and green chilies, and the chicken-broth base is enriched with milk.

¼ cup butter or margarine
1 onion, chopped
1 red sweet pepper, seeded and chopped

•••

6 tablespoons all-purpose flour
2 14½-ounce cans chicken broth

•••

1 17-ounce can whole kernel corn, drained
1 4-ounce can diced green chili peppers, drained
1 teaspoon dry mustard
1 teaspoon ground cumin
½ cup milk

Melt the butter or margarine in a large saucepan. Add the onion and red sweet pepper. Cook over medium heat until onion and pepper are tender.

Add the flour and cook for about 2 minutes, stirring constantly. Gradually stir in the chicken broth, using a wire whisk to break up any lumps.

Add the corn, green chilies, dry mustard, and cumin. Bring the soup to boiling, stirring constantly. Add the milk, reduce heat to low, and simmer, uncovered, for 20 minutes, stirring occasionally.

Makes 6 side-dish servings

Per serving: 207 calories, 5 g protein, 27 g carbohydrate, 10 g total fat (2 g saturated), 2 mg cholesterol, 1,114 mg sodium, 398 mg potassium

Potato Soup with Leeks and Carrot

There are many versions of potato soup, but adding leeks, carrot, and dill gives an old favorite more flavor and color. Serve with French bread sliced in half, topped with cheddar cheese, and toasted under the broiler.

2 leeks

•••

2 tablespoons butter or margarine
1 carrot, chopped

4 large red potatoes (about 2 pounds), peeled and cut into ½-inch cubes
2 cups water
1 teaspoon salt

•••

2 cups milk
¼ teaspoon dried dillweed or ¾ teaspoon snipped fresh dillweed
⅛ teaspoon pepper

To prepare the leeks, peel away any dry outer leaves. Cut off the green tops about 1 inch above the white section and remove the roots. To remove any sand, slice the leek in half lengthwise, and rinse each half thoroughly under cold running water. Shake off excess water, and thinly slice the leek.

Melt the butter or margarine in a large saucepan or Dutch oven over low heat. Add the leek and carrot and cook slowly, stirring often, for 5 minutes.

Add the potatoes, water, and salt, and heat to boiling. Boil gently, uncovered, over medium-high heat until the potatoes are tender (about 12 minutes). Stir occasionally to avoid sticking.

With a potato masher or the back of a large spoon, coarsely mash the potatoes just enough to thicken the soup. Add the milk, dillweed, and pepper; heat through. Season to taste.

Makes 4 side-dish servings

Per serving: 270 calories, 7 g protein, 43 g carbohydrate, 8 g total fat (5 g saturated), 25 mg cholesterol, 670 mg sodium, 813 mg potassium

Tomato-Basil Bean Soup

Baking the beans gives them a hearty, roasted flavor.

1 pound dry pinto or great northern beans

•••

2 tablespoons olive oil
½ cup chopped onion
½ cup thinly sliced celery
3 cloves garlic, minced
1 14½-ounce can Italian tomatoes, cut up
2 teaspoons dried basil, crushed, or 2 tablespoons snipped fresh basil
1 teaspoon salt
½ teaspoon pepper

•••

Grated Parmesan cheese (optional)

Sort and wash the beans. Place them in a large bowl, cover with cold water, and soak for 8 hours or overnight. Drain the water from the beans, and place them in a large ovenproof pot or Dutch oven. (Or, combine the beans and 8 cups cold water in a large ovenproof pot or Dutch oven. Bring to boiling; reduce heat. Simmer for 2 minutes; remove from heat. Cover and let stand for 1 hour.)

Drain and rinse the beans. Add 4 cups fresh cold water to the beans. Cover and bake in a 350° oven for 1½ hours or until the beans are tender.

Meanwhile, heat the olive oil in a large skillet over low heat. Add the onion, celery, and garlic, and cook until tender. Add the mixture to the pot of beans. Stir in the tomatoes, basil, salt, and pepper. Return the pot to the oven, and bake 30 minutes longer to blend flavors. If the soup appears to be too thick, stir in ½ cup water.

If desired, sprinkle grated Parmesan cheese over the soup before serving.

Makes 6 side-dish servings

Per serving: 167 calories, 7 g protein, 25 g carbohydrate, 5 g total fat (1 g saturated), 0 mg cholesterol, 471 mg sodium, 565 mg potassium

Golden Vegetable Soup

When a quick and nourishing soup is desired, transform a few vegetables, herbs, and chicken broth into a delicate pureed soup in about an hour. If fresh beans aren't available, substitute drained, canned yellow wax or green beans.

¼ cup butter or margarine
1 large onion, peeled and chopped
   (1 cup)
2 celery stalks, chopped (1 cup)
1 large carrot, peeled and chopped
   (¾ cup)
1 large potato, peeled and chopped
   (1¼ cups)
¼ pound yellow wax or green beans,
   ends removed and thinly sliced
   (1 cup)
1 clove garlic, peeled

••••

3 cups chicken broth
1 teaspoon snipped fresh marjoram or
   ¼ teaspoon dried marjoram,
   crushed
1 teaspoon snipped fresh tarragon or
   ¼ teaspoon dried tarragon, crushed
1 teaspoon snipped fresh dillweed or
   ⅛ teaspoon dried dillweed
½ cup milk
   Salt
   Pepper

••••

Dairy sour cream

Melt the butter or margarine over low heat in a large saucepan. Add the onion, celery, carrot, potato, beans, and garlic. Cook over low heat, stirring occasionally, for 20 to 25 minutes or until tender but not brown.

Add the chicken broth, marjoram, tarragon, and dillweed. Bring to boiling; reduce heat. Simmer, uncovered, for 30 minutes or until all vegetables are very tender. Carefully pour the hot soup into a blender or food processor. Cover and blend or process until smooth. (If using a food processor, process half at a time.) Return soup to the pan, and add the milk. Heat through; add salt and pepper to taste.

Serve hot, garnished with a dollop of sour cream.

Makes 4 to 6 side-dish servings

Per serving: 249 calories, 5 g protein, 22 g carbohydrate, 17 g total fat (10 g saturated), 40 mg cholesterol, 942 mg sodium, 623 mg potassium

Vegetarian Chili

Complete this meatless meal with a whole grain roll and some shredded cheese on top of the chili. To lower the chili's sodium, use canned tomatoes with no salt added and rinse and drain the canned beans before adding them.

2 tablespoons olive oil
1 large onion, chopped (¾ cup)
2 cloves garlic, chopped
2 yellow summer squash, thinly sliced

•••

1 Anaheim pepper, seeded and chopped
1 green sweet pepper, seeded and chopped (¾ cup)
1 red sweet pepper, seeded and chopped (¾ cup)
1 carrot, peeled and chopped into ¼-inch pieces

•••

1 tablespoon chili powder
1 teaspoon ground cumin
½ teaspoon salt
⅛ to ¼ teaspoon crushed red pepper

•••

1 14½-ounce can stewed tomatoes
1 15-ounce can red beans
1 15-ounce can black beans, rinsed and drained

Heat the olive oil in a large saucepan or Dutch oven over medium heat. Add the onion, garlic, and squash, and cook just until tender (about 5 minutes).

Add the Anaheim pepper, green and red sweet peppers, and carrot. Cook, stirring occasionally, for 5 to 8 minutes or until peppers are crisp-tender.

Add the chili powder, cumin, salt, and crushed red pepper, and cook, stirring gently, for 1 minute.

Add the tomatoes and red and black beans. Bring to boiling; reduce heat. Simmer, uncovered, for 20 minutes, stirring occasionally.

Makes 4 main-dish or 6 side-dish servings

Per serving: 288 calories, 15 g protein, 48 g carbohydrate, 9 g total fat (1 g saturated), 0 mg cholesterol, 1,147 mg sodium, 1,075 mg potassium

Sambhar Chicken Stew

Sambhar powder is a combination of red chilies, turmeric, cumin, coriander, mustard seeds, and other spices used in Indian cooking. It adds a robust, spicy flavor to this chicken stew. Sambhar powder can be purchased at health food stores or at specialty stores that carry Indian spices.

1 2½- to 3-pound whole broiler-fryer chicken
1 stalk celery, halved crosswise
1 medium carrot, halved crosswise
1 small onion, sliced in half
1 teaspoon salt
¼ teaspoon pepper

•••

1 teaspoon cumin seed
1 teaspoon mustard seed

•••

3 tablespoons olive oil
1 medium onion, chopped (½ cup)
1 medium green sweet pepper, seeded and chopped (½ cup)
2 cloves garlic, minced

•••

2 small yellow squash, quartered lengthwise and sliced ¼ inch thick (1½ cups)
2 small zucchini, quartered lengthwise and sliced ¼ inch thick (1½ cups)

•••

2 14½-ounce cans tomatoes, undrained and cut up
1 to 2 tablespoons Sambhar powder or curry powder
3 ounces macaroni

Place the chicken in a large pot or 6- to 8-quart Dutch oven. Add the celery, carrot, halved onion, salt, pepper, and enough water to cover (about 6 cups). Bring to boiling; reduce heat. Cover and simmer for 1 hour or until the chicken is tender and no pink remains. Remove the chicken from the pan. When cool enough to handle, remove the meat from the bones; discard skin and bones. Cut the meat into bite-size pieces; set aside. Strain the broth, discarding the vegetables. Skim off the fat, measure 4 cups of chicken broth, and reserve.

In a small skillet, toast the cumin and mustard seeds over low heat for 2 to 3 minutes or until lightly browned, stirring often. Cool seeds and coarsely crush in a mortar with pestle; set aside.

Heat the olive oil over low heat in the large pot or Dutch oven. Add the chopped onion, chopped green pepper, and garlic, stirring occasionally until tender.

Add the crushed cumin and mustard seeds, yellow squash, and zucchini. Cook and stir over medium-high heat for 3 to 5 minutes or until squash and zucchini are crisp-tender.

Add the 4 cups reserved chicken broth, the undrained tomatoes, Sambhar or curry powder, and macaroni. Bring to boiling; reduce heat. Simmer, uncovered, for 8 to 10 minutes or until the macaroni is tender. Add chicken and heat through.

Makes 6 to 8 main-dish servings

Per serving: 473 calories, 38 g protein, 24 g carbohydrate, 25 g total fat (6 g saturated), 108 mg cholesterol, 694 mg sodium, 877 mg potassium

Beef Stew

Traditional beef stew seems to create its own warmth on a wintery day. It takes time to prepare, but you'll be glad you made the effort. In this version of the timeless favorite, the meat and gravy are served over boiled potatoes. If you prefer, you can add the potatoes to the meat mixture with the carrots and celery to cook until tender.

2 to 3 pounds beef chuck or shoulder roast
½ cup all-purpose flour
•••
3 tablespoons butter or margarine
2 tablespoons cooking oil
1 onion, chopped (½ cup)
1 14½-ounce can beef broth
2 cups water
1 teaspoon salt
½ teaspoon dried thyme, crushed
½ teaspoon dried basil, crushed
½ teaspoon dried tarragon, crushed
½ teaspoon dried rosemary, crushed
1 bay leaf
•••
4 large carrots, peeled and chopped into 1-inch pieces
2 celery sticks, chopped into 1-inch pieces
•••
4 large potatoes, peeled and chopped into 1-inch pieces
•••
3 tablespoons all-purpose flour
¼ cup water
•••
1 8¾-ounce can corn, drained

Remove excess fat from the meat; cut into 1-inch cubes. Place the ½ cup flour in a plastic bag. Add meat cubes, a few at a time, shaking to coat meat with flour.

Heat about half of the butter or margarine and half of the oil in a Dutch oven over medium-high heat. Add the meat, half at a time, and brown, turning often to brown evenly (about 8 to 10 minutes). Repeat with remaining butter, oil, and meat. If necessary, drain off any excess fat. Return all meat to the Dutch oven.

Add the onion and ¼ cup of the beef broth to the hot Dutch oven, and scrape up the brown bits.

Add the remaining beef broth, the 2 cups water, the salt, thyme, basil, tarragon, rosemary, and bay leaf. Bring to boiling; reduce heat. Cover and simmer for 1 hour.

Add the carrots and celery. Cover and simmer for 30 to 40 minutes or until they are tender.

Meanwhile, boil the potatoes in a large pot of water, covered, about 20 minutes or until they are tender. Drain and keep warm.

Combine the 3 tablespoons flour and the ¼ cup water; add to meat mixture. Cook and stir until thickened and bubbly. Add corn; cook 1 minute more.

To serve, place the potatoes in individual bowls and ladle the stew on top.

Makes 6 to 8 main-dish servings

Per serving: 531 calories, 43 g protein, 43 g carbohydrate, 21 g total fat (8 g saturated), 130 mg cholesterol, 813 mg sodium, 995 mg potassium

Lime Soup

As a first course with your favorite Mexican meal, you'll find this soup uncommonly refreshing. Or, serve it with a crisp green salad as a light summer entrée.

1 tablespoon butter or margarine
1 tablespoon olive oil
1 large onion, thinly sliced
    (about 1 cup)
1 cup thinly sliced celery
4 large bone-in chicken breast halves
    (2 pounds total)
3 14½-ounce cans chicken broth

•••

2 cloves garlic, peeled
1 teaspoon chili powder
½ teaspoon ground cumin
¼ teaspoon crushed red pepper

•••

3 tomatoes, peeled and chopped
4 to 6 tablespoons lime juice
    Salt
    Pepper

•••

Tortilla chips, or 4 corn tortillas, cut
    into ½-inch strips and fried until
    crisp

Heat the butter or margarine and olive oil in a large saucepan or Dutch oven. Add the onion and celery, and cook over medium-low heat until tender.

Rinse chicken breasts; pat dry with paper towels. Add the chicken breasts and broth to vegetables. Bring to boiling; reduce heat. Simmer, uncovered, until the chicken is tender (about 20 minutes). Remove the chicken from the broth. When cool enough to handle, remove meat from bones. Discard skin and bones. Cut the chicken into strips or bite-size pieces (you should have about 2 cups).

Return the chicken meat to the pan, and add the garlic, chili powder, cumin, and crushed red pepper. Return to boiling; reduce heat. Simmer, uncovered, for 20 minutes.

Remove the garlic cloves from the soup. Add the tomatoes and lime juice and heat through. Season to taste with salt and pepper. Serve with the tortilla chips or fried tortilla strips.

Makes 4 main-dish servings

Per serving: 266 calories, 26 g protein, 13 g carbohydrate, 13 g total fat (4 g saturated), 67 mg cholesterol, 1,504 mg sodium, 813 mg potassium

Secret Chili

This rich, spicy chili is ready in minutes. The secret is the unexpected zing of cinnamon and cloves; it will have your guests begging for the recipe.

1 pound ground beef
1 medium onion, finely chopped
    (½ cup)
2 cloves garlic, minced

● ● ●

2 tablespoons chili powder
1 teaspoon ground cinnamon
½ teaspoon ground cloves
½ teaspoon ground cumin
¼ teaspoon salt

● ● ●

1 15-ounce can chili beans with chili
    gravy
1 14½-ounce can whole tomatoes
1 8-ounce can tomato sauce

● ● ●

Hot cooked pasta (optional)
Shredded cheddar cheese (optional)
Chopped onion (optional)

In a large skillet or 3-quart saucepan, brown the ground beef with the onion and garlic. Drain off fat.

Add the chili powder, cinnamon, cloves, cumin, and salt.

Add the beans, tomatoes, and tomato sauce. Simmer, uncovered, for about 20 minutes to blend flavors. If desired, serve over hot cooked pasta and sprinkle with cheese and onions.

Makes 4 to 6 main-dish servings

Per serving: 407 calories, 33 g protein, 26 g carbohydrate, 20 g total fat (8 g saturated), 102 mg cholesterol, 1,308 mg sodium, 1,258 mg potassium

Starch Supports......

Are you looking for a new way to prepare those old standbys, potatoes or rice? The recipes here can make a family dinner special or highlight a dinner-party menu.

New Potatoes with Rosemary

In addition to rosemary, basil, thyme, or dillweed can complement this saucy potato side dish.

1½ **pounds whole tiny new potatoes**

•••

2 **tablespoons butter or margarine**
1 **large onion, thinly sliced into rings**
3 **large cloves garlic, minced**

•••

½ **teaspoon dried rosemary, crushed**
⅔ **cup chicken broth**
  Salt
  Pepper

In a large saucepan, cover the potatoes with cold water. Bring to a gentle boil over medium-high heat. Cook for 8 to 10 minutes or just until the potatoes begin to soften, but are not thoroughly cooked. Drain the potatoes, and rinse them with cold water. Slice the potatoes in half; set aside.

Melt the butter or margarine over medium heat in a large skillet. Add the onion and garlic and cook, stirring often, until tender and lightly brown.

Add the potatoes and rosemary. Pour the chicken broth over the potatoes. Bring to boiling; reduce heat. Cover and simmer for 10 to 15 minutes or until the potatoes are tender. Uncover and cook for 2 to 3 minutes more or until most of the liquid is evaporated. Sprinkle with salt and pepper to taste.

Serves 6

Per serving: 165 calories, 3 g protein, 29 g carbohydrate, 4 g total fat (2 g saturated), 10 mg cholesterol, 201 mg sodium, 559 mg potassium

Potatoes Parisian

Potatoes Parisian is one of the most elegant (and simplest) ways to prepare potatoes. This versatile starch side goes with almost any entrée. Bon appétit!

3 large potatoes, peeled and thinly
    sliced (1½ pounds)
1½ cups whipping cream
½ teaspoon salt
½ cup shredded Gruyère cheese
    (2 ounces)
    Ground nutmeg

Place the sliced potatoes in a buttered 3-quart rectangular baking dish. Pour the whipping cream over the potatoes. Sprinkle with salt.

Bake, uncovered, in a 350° oven for 50 to 60 minutes or until the potatoes are tender and most of the cream is absorbed. Sprinkle with shredded cheese and nutmeg for the last 5 minutes of cooking.

Serves 6

Per serving: 348 calories, 6 g protein, 24 g carbohydrate, 26 g total fat (16 g saturated), 94 mg cholesterol, 243 mg sodium, 424 mg potassium

Frank's German Potato Salad

The addition of chopped apples makes this German-style potato salad unique. It has a sweet and sour taste that brightens up a meal. Serve with pork or chicken, or take it along to a potluck dinner.

4 strips bacon

•••

4 large potatoes, peeled and cut into ½-inch cubes (4 cups)
1 small onion, chopped (¼ cup)

•••

½ cup cider vinegar
½ cup water
¼ cup sugar
1 red apple, unpeeled and chopped into bite-size pieces
Fresh parsley

Fry the bacon until crisp in a large skillet over medium heat. Drain on paper towels, reserving drippings in skillet. Crumble bacon and set aside.

Add the potatoes and onion to the reserved drippings in the skillet. Cook over medium heat until the potatoes are lightly browned, but still firm, and the onion is tender (15 to 20 minutes). With a slotted spoon, transfer the potatoes and onion to a large bowl, reserving the drippings in the skillet.

Add the vinegar, water, and sugar to the skillet; stir to mix. Add the apples. Bring to boiling; boil for 1 minute. Pour the sauce over the potatoes and onion. Add the crumbled bacon and toss gently until well blended. Cool to room temperature, stirring occasionally, allowing the flavors to mellow and the potatoes to absorb some of the liquid. Garnish with parsley.

Serves 4 to 6

Per serving: 309 calories, 6 g protein, 66 g carbohydrate, 4 g total fat (1 g saturated), 5 mg cholesterol, 114 mg sodium, 867 mg potassium

Dutch Potatoes

This colorful dish is an easy meal-in-one. Chances are, you have all the ingredients on hand. Serve it for breakfast, lunch, or dinner.

6 strips bacon
2 pounds potatoes, peeled and cut up
1 medium onion, finely chopped
2 eggs
2 medium tomatoes, chopped
½ cup chopped sweet pickle
Salt
Pepper

Fry bacon until crisp in a large skillet over medium heat. Drain bacon on paper towels, reserving the drippings in a glass measure. Crumble bacon into small pieces and set aside.

Return 3 tablespoons bacon drippings to skillet (add additional drippings as necessary while cooking). Add the potatoes and onion to the drippings in the skillet. Cook, covered, over medium-low heat about 12 minutes or until the onion and potatoes are tender and lightly brown, turning occasionally. Transfer the potatoes and onion to a large bowl, reserving the drippings in the skillet.

Add the the eggs (yolks unbroken) to the skillet, and cook until the yolks are soft set (over easy). Remove eggs from the skillet.

To assemble, add the crumbled bacon, eggs, tomatoes, and pickles to the bowl of potatoes and onions. Fold the ingredients together, breaking eggs into bite-size pieces and allowing the soft yolks to coat the other ingredients. Add salt and pepper to taste.

Serves 6

Per serving: 192 calories, 6 g protein, 32 g carbohydrate, 5 g total fat (2 g saturated), 76 mg cholesterol, 350 mg sodium, 502 mg potassium

Gnocchi with Herb-Tomato Sauce

These potato dumplings are delicious served with meat or fish or as the starter course of a special meal. The Herb-Tomato Sauce may be made ahead. Simply cover and chill the sauce after it is blended. Reheat, adding the cream and thickening the sauce, just before serving.

Herb-Tomato Sauce:

2 tablespoons butter or margarine
½ cup chopped onion
2 cloves garlic, chopped
1 14½-ounce can Italian plum
    tomatoes, undrained
½ cup chicken broth
½ cup dry white wine
¼ teaspoon dried basil, crushed, or
    1 teaspoon snipped fresh basil
¼ teaspoon dried tarragon, crushed, or
    1 teaspoon snipped fresh tarragon
¼ teaspoon dried oregano, crushed, or
    1 teaspoon snipped fresh oregano
¼ teaspoon dried marjoram, crushed, or
    1 teaspoon snipped fresh marjoram
¼ teaspoon salt
¼ teaspoon sugar
½ cup whipping cream

Gnocchi:

1 pound red potatoes, peeled and
    quartered
½ teaspoon salt
1 egg, beaten
1 to 1½ cups all-purpose flour

•••

Grated Parmesan cheese

Herb-Tomato Sauce: Heat the butter or margarine over low heat in a large skillet. Add the onion and garlic. Cook about 5 minutes or until tender but not brown.

Add the undrained tomatoes, breaking them up slightly, and the chicken broth, wine, basil, tarragon, oregano, marjoram, salt, and sugar. Boil gently over medium-low heat, stirring occasionally, until the sauce is reduced by half (12 to 15 minutes).

Pour the sauce into a blender container or food processor bowl and blend or process until smooth. Return the sauce to the skillet. Add the cream, and simmer over low heat until slightly thickened (about 5 minutes).

Gnocchi: Cook the potatoes in a large amount of boiling water until tender (15 to 20 minutes). Drain and mash thoroughly in a large bowl. Add salt and cool to room temperature.

Add egg to potato mixture. Gradually mix in as much of the flour as needed to form a soft dough. Divide the dough in half. On a floured surface, roll each half of the dough into a sausage-like roll about 1 inch in diameter. Slice the dough into ¾-inch pieces. With a fork, make a slight indentation in one side of each piece. (This helps the sauce to cling to the gnocchi.)

Drop the dough pieces into a large saucepan or Dutch oven of boiling water. When they float to the surface (after about 5 to 8 minutes), cook them for 10 seconds more, then quickly remove them with a slotted spoon. Place gnocchi on a heated platter. Serve the warm tomato sauce over gnocchi and top with Parmesan cheese.

Serves 6 to 8

Per serving: 321 calories, 9 g protein, 37 g carbohydrate, 15 g total fat (9 g saturated), 78 mg cholesterol, 637 mg sodium, 499 mg potassium

Orange-Cumin Couscous

Couscous is both a tiny pasta and a traditional North African dish that features the pasta. This version of the dish is flavored with orange juice, cinnamon, almonds, and raisins.

¼ teaspoon cumin seed

•••

¾ cup chicken broth or water
¼ cup orange juice
½ cup couscous

•••

2 tablespoons butter or margarine
¼ cup sliced almonds
   Pinch of cinnamon
2 tablespoons golden raisins, chopped

Toast the cumin seed in a small skillet over low heat, turning it often, until lightly brown (2 to 3 minutes). Cool and crush in a mortar with pestle.

In a medium saucepan, combine the chicken broth or water and orange juice, and bring to boiling over high heat. Stir in the couscous and toasted cumin seed and return to boiling. Cover the pan, and remove it from the heat. Let stand about 10 minutes to allow the couscous to absorb the liquid.

Meanwhile, melt the butter or margarine in a large skillet over medium heat. Stir in the almonds and cinnamon and cook about 5 minutes or until the butter is golden and the nuts are toasted. Lower the heat if the butter begins to brown too soon. Add the raisins. Spoon the couscous loosely into the skillet. Let the couscous brown lightly for about 5 minutes. Turn and continue browning for 5 minutes more.

Serves 4

Per serving: 187 calories, 4 g protein, 23 g carbohydrate, 9 g total fat (4 g saturated), 16 mg cholesterol, 243 mg sodium, 238 mg potassium

Rice Pilaf

Elegant, yet easy to prepare, rice pilaf goes well with almost any entrée. Onion, garlic, cheese, and chicken broth add richness to this pleasing side dish.

3 tablespoons butter or margarine
1 onion, finely chopped
2 cloves garlic, minced
1 cup long grain rice
2 cups chicken broth
¼ cup shredded Gruyère cheese
Fresh snipped parsley

Melt the butter or margarine in a medium saucepan over medium-low heat. Add the onion and garlic. Cook, stirring occasionally, until onion is tender. Add the rice and continue cooking, stirring often, for 3 to 5 minutes or until rice begins to brown. Carefully stir in the chicken broth. Bring to boiling; reduce heat. Cover and simmer for 15 to 20 minutes or until liquid is absorbed and rice is tender. Remove from heat, and stir in cheese. Sprinkle with parsley.

Serves 4 to 6

Per serving: 305 calories, 7 g protein, 40 g carbohydrate, 13 g total fat (7 g saturated), 32 mg cholesterol, 599 mg sodium, 194 mg potassium

Wild and Brown Rice Pilaf

The combination of wild rice and brown rice makes a distinctive side dish for grilled meats or fowl.

½ cup wild rice
½ cup brown rice

•••

2 tablespoons butter or margarine
1 cup chopped onion
2¾ cups beef broth
½ teaspoon dried thyme, crushed, or
    2 teaspoons snipped fresh thyme

Rinse the wild rice and brown rice in cold water; drain well.

Melt the butter or margarine in a large saucepan over medium-low heat. Add the onion and cook until tender. Add the rice and cook for 3 minutes, stirring frequently. Stir in the beef broth and thyme. Bring to boiling; reduce heat. Cover and cook for about 45 minutes or until rice is tender and liquid is absorbed. If necessary, uncover and simmer about 5 minutes to reduce liquid, stirring occasionally.

Serves 4 to 6

Per serving: 232 calories, 7 g protein, 37 g carbohydrate, 7 g total fat (4 g saturated), 16 mg cholesterol, 734 mg sodium, 250 mg potassium

Italian Rice with Saffron and Carrots

This rich and creamy side dish, made with Arborio rice, goes well with chicken or fish. You can find Arborio rice in an Italian market or in the specialty foods section of some supermarkets.

2 tablespoons butter or margarine
1 cup finely chopped onion
1 clove garlic, minced

• • •

2½ cups chicken broth
1 cup Arborio rice or long grain rice
1 cup sliced carrots
½ cup dry white wine
⅛ teaspoon ground saffron or crushed
   saffron threads
¼ teaspoon salt

Melt the butter or margarine over medium heat in a large saucepan. Add the onion and garlic. Cook slowly, stirring occasionally, until the onions are tender.

Add the chicken broth, rice, carrots, white wine, saffron, and salt. Bring to boiling; reduce heat. Cover and simmer for 15 minutes or until rice is tender and most of the liquid is absorbed. Remove the pan from heat, and let rice stand for 5 minutes before serving.

Serves 6

Per serving: 194 calories, 4 g protein, 30 g carbohydrate, 5 g total fat (3 g saturated), 10 mg cholesterol, 540 mg sodium, 249 mg potassium

You can prepare the stuffed chard leaves up to 24 hours ahead, then cover and chill. Add the bundles to the baking dish along with the hot Dill Sauce and bake in a 350° oven for 40 minutes or until the bundles are heated through.

2 cups water
1 cup basmati rice or long grain rice
½ teaspoon salt

•••

16 large chard or cabbage leaves
(stems removed)

Rice Filling:

1 egg, slightly beaten
¼ cup milk
1 tablespoon cooking oil
½ teaspoon finely shredded lemon peel
2 teaspoons lemon juice
¼ teaspoon dried dillweed
⅛ teaspoon white pepper
1 cup finely chopped fresh spinach
½ cup shredded cheddar cheese
(2 ounces)
¼ cup finely chopped onion
2 cloves garlic, minced

Dill Sauce:

¼ cup butter or margarine
¼ cup all-purpose flour
1½ cups milk
½ teaspoon dried dillweed
⅛ teaspoon white pepper
¼ cup dry white wine

Bring the water to boiling over high heat in a medium saucepan. Add the rice and salt. Return to boiling; reduce heat. Cover and simmer for about 15 minutes or until rice is tender and liquid is absorbed. Remove from the heat and let stand, covered, for 5 to 10 minutes.

Meanwhile, bring a large pan of water to boiling. Dip the chard or cabbage leaves in the boiling water for a few seconds; remove leaves with tongs and plunge them into a bowl of ice water. Drain well on paper towels; set aside.

Rice Filling: In a large bowl, combine the egg, milk, oil, lemon peel, lemon juice, dillweed, and white pepper. Stir in cooked rice, spinach, cheese, onion, and garlic. Place each chard or cabbage leaf on a flat surface, vein side up. Place about ¼ cup of the rice filling on each leaf; roll up, tucking in the sides.

Dill Sauce: Melt butter or margarine over low heat in a medium saucepan. Add the flour and blend thoroughly. Stir in the milk all at once. Add the dillweed and white pepper. Cook over medium heat, stirring constantly, until sauce is thickened and bubbly. Stir in the wine.

Spread 1 cup of the sauce over the bottom of a 3-quart rectangular baking dish. Place rice-stuffed leaves, seam sides down, in the baking dish. Spoon the remaining Dill Sauce over the leaves. Cover and bake in a 350° oven for 30 minutes or until heated through.

Serves 8

Per serving: 247 calories, 7 g protein, 27 g carbohydrate, 12 g total fat (6 g saturated), 54 mg cholesterol, 286 mg sodium, 284 mg potassium

A Vegetable A Day

Whether garden-fresh or frozen, vegetables are a wise choice to complete a meal. Try one of our cream-of-the-crop recipes or create your own with our suggestions in Vegetable Dress-Ups.

Vegetable Festival

Loaded with color and flavor, this vegetable combination can be served at room temperature or chilled. Allow several hours for the vegetables to chill thoroughly and serve on leaf lettuce or Bibb lettuce leaves.

1 tablespoon olive oil
1 medium onion, cut into ½-inch pieces
1 clove garlic, minced
1 medium carrot, cut into ¼-inch pieces (½ cup)
1 medium yellow summer squash, halved lengthwise and thinly sliced (2 cups)
2 Anaheim peppers, seeded and thinly sliced (⅔ cup)
1 large red sweet pepper, cut into ¼-inch pieces (1¼ cups)

Rice Vinaigrette:
2 tablespoons rice vinegar
⅛ teaspoon salt
3 tablespoons olive oil

Heat the 1 tablespoon olive oil over medium heat in a 10-inch skillet. Add the onion, garlic, and carrot. Cook for 5 minutes, stirring frequently. Add the squash and peppers. Cook about 5 minutes more, stirring often, until vegetables are crisp-tender. Spoon the vegetables into a bowl.

Rice Vinaigrette: Combine the vinegar and salt in a small bowl. Whisk in the olive oil.

Pour the vinaigrette over the vegetables, and stir gently to combine. Serve at room temperature.

Serves 4

Per serving: 168 calories, 2 g protein, 11 g carbohydrate, 14 g total fat (2 g saturated), 0 mg cholesterol, 79 mg sodium, 394 mg potassium

Golden Glazed Carrots

When preparing this recipe, use young, fresh carrots from the garden whenever possible. This cooking method brings out their deliciously sweet flavor.

6 medium carrots, cut into ½-inch slices
¼ cup water
2 tablespoons butter or margarine
1 teaspoon snipped fresh thyme or
    ¼ teaspoon dried thyme, crushed
1 teaspoon sugar
¼ teaspoon salt

In a medium skillet, combine the carrots, water, butter or margarine, thyme, sugar, and salt. Bring to boiling; reduce heat. Cover and simmer for 10 to 15 minutes or until the carrots are crisp-tender and most of the liquid has been absorbed.

Remove the lid and increase the heat to medium high. Continue cooking the carrots until most of the liquid has evaporated (about 4 minutes). Lower the heat and cook about 3 minutes more or until the carrots are glazed, shaking the pan often.

Serves 4

Per serving: 102 calories, 1 g protein, 12 g carbohydrate, 6 g total fat (4 g saturated), 16 mg cholesterol, 230 mg sodium, 351 mg potassium

Glazed Yellow Squash

Perk up yellow squash with the flavors of cinnamon, brown sugar, and almonds. This slightly sweet vegetable dish goes well with grilled meats.

2 tablespoons butter or margarine
5 cups thinly sliced yellow summer
    squash

•••

¼ teaspoon salt
1 tablespoon brown sugar
⅛ teaspoon ground cinnamon
2 tablespoons sliced almonds

Melt the butter or margarine in a large skillet. Add the squash and cook over medium heat for about 5 minutes, turning occasionally, until the squash is tender and its edges begin to brown.

Sprinkle squash with salt. Add the brown sugar, cinnamon, and almonds. Stir gently until the brown sugar dissolves and the mixture is bubbly.

Serves 4

Per serving: 108 calories, 2 g protein, 9 g carbohydrate, 8 g total fat (4 g saturated), 16 mg cholesterol, 196 mg sodium, 377 mg potassium

Snow Peas, Carrots, and Onion

Serve this pretty vegetable dish in late spring when these vegetables are at their best.

2 tablespoons butter or margarine
1 cup chopped onion
2 medium carrots, thinly sliced (1 cup)
8 ounces snow peas
1 tablespoon snipped fresh dillweed or
    1 teaspoon dried dillweed

Melt the butter or margarine in a large skillet over medium heat. Add the chopped onion. Cook until tender, stirring occasionally. Increase heat to medium-high and add the carrots. Cook for 2 minutes. Add the snow peas. Cook and stir for 2 to 3 minutes or until the snow peas are crisp-tender. Sprinkle with dillweed and toss.

Serves 4

Per serving: 107 calories, 3 g protein, 12 g carbohydrate, 6 g total fat (4 g saturated), 16 mg cholesterol, 88 mg sodium, 268 mg potassium

Corn and Broccoli Casserole

The colorful duo of corn and broccoli makes an easy-to-prepare casserole for your next potluck party or holiday dinner. It pairs well with roast turkey or ham.

1 10-ounce package frozen cut broccoli, thawed and drained
1 10-ounce package frozen whole kernel corn, thawed and drained
½ cup coarsely crushed rich round crackers
½ cup shredded cheddar cheese (2 ounces)
½ cup whipping cream or half-and-half
1 egg, beaten
2 tablespoons butter or margarine, melted
½ teaspoon onion powder
¼ teaspoon salt
⅛ teaspoon garlic powder
⅛ teaspoon pepper

Crumb Topping
½ cup coarsely crushed rich round crackers
2 tablespoons butter or margarine, melted

Place the broccoli and corn in a large bowl. Add the crushed crackers, cheese, whipping cream or half-and-half, egg, butter or margarine, onion powder, salt, garlic powder, and pepper. Stir to combine the mixture. Spoon the mixture into a 1½-quart round casserole or a 9-inch pie plate.

Crumb Topping: Sprinkle crushed crackers evenly over casserole. Drizzle with melted butter or margarine.

Bake, uncovered, in a 350° oven for about 25 minutes or until the edges are bubbly.

Serves 6

Per serving: 230 calories, 7 g protein, 16 g carbohydrate, 17 g total fat (9 g saturated), 83 mg cholesterol, 261 mg sodium, 185 mg potassium

Corn-Stuffed Plum Tomatoes

Plum tomatoes, also known as Italian tomatoes, are thick and meaty with small seeds, little juice, and a mild, flavor.

8 Italian plum tomatoes

•••

2 tablespoons olive oil
1 cup finely chopped onion
¼ cup finely chopped green sweet
    pepper
4 cloves garlic, minced
1 cup cooked fresh or frozen whole
    kernel corn or 1 cup canned whole
    kernel corn, drained
2 tablespoons snipped fresh basil
¼ cup fine dry bread crumbs
¼ cup shredded sharp (aged) provolone
    cheese
   Dash salt
   Dash white pepper

Slice the tomatoes in half lengthwise. With a small spoon, scoop out the seeds and membranes, leaving ¼-inch-thick shells. Invert on paper towels to drain; set aside.

Heat the olive oil over medium-low heat in a medium skillet. Add the onion, green pepper, and garlic. Cook for about 5 minutes, stirring often, until the onion and pepper are tender. Add the corn, and cook for 1 minute more. Remove the pan from the heat, and stir in the basil, bread crumbs, and cheese. Add salt and white pepper. Spoon the mixture into the tomato halves.

Place the tomatoes in a shallow baking pan. Bake, uncovered, in a 350° oven for 8 to 10 minutes or until the tomatoes are tender and the stuffing is heated through.

Or, if desired, grill the tomatoes. Place a piece of aluminum foil large enough to hold the tomatoes on the grill directly over medium coals. Place the tomatoes on the foil. Grill, uncovered, for 8 to 10 minutes or until the tomatoes are tender and the stuffing is heated through. Carefully remove the tomatoes from the grill with a large metal spatula, spoon, or tongs.

Serves 4

Per serving: 209 calories, 6 g protein, 27 g carbohydrate, 10 g total fat (3 g saturated), 6 mg cholesterol, 179 mg sodium, 534 mg potassium

Vegetable Dress-Ups

Dress up your plain vegetables! We suggest the ingredients; the exact amounts are left up to your good taste.

Asparagus

Wash asparagus spears. Scrape off scales and break off woody bases where spears break easily. Boil until tender (4 to 8 minutes) and drain. Melt butter or margarine and squeeze in fresh orange juice to taste. Pour over asparagus and garnish with finely shredded orange peel.

Broccoli

Wash fresh broccoli; remove outer leaves and tough parts of stalks. Steam or boil broccoli (8 to 12 minutes) and serve with melted butter or margarine. Garnish with lemon wedges or sprinkle finely shredded cheddar or Swiss cheese on the broccoli just before serving.

Carrots

Scrub baby carrots and boil in a small amount of water or chicken broth until tender; drain. Sauté in melted butter or margarine. Remove from heat. Carefully pour a small amount of brandy over the carrots and set aflame or simmer 1 minute. Garnish with fresh, chopped parsley.

Corn

Cook a small, chopped onion in butter or margarine until tender. Add a chopped, fresh tomato and 2 cups of cooked or canned whole kernel corn, drained. Cover and simmer until tomato is tender (3 to 4 minutes). Stir in chili powder to taste. Garnish with a dollop of sour cream and chopped cilantro.

Green Beans

Steam fresh or frozen green beans until crisp-tender. Serve with lemon wedges and melted butter or margarine.

Mushrooms

Slice fresh mushrooms and fry quickly in butter or margarine over medium-high heat for about 4 minutes or until tender. Add freshly squeezed lemon juice and a pinch of thyme while cooking.

New Potatoes

Wash new potatoes; steam them about 20 minutes or until tender. Transfer potatoes to a bowl. Drizzle with melted butter or margarine, and garnish with a sprinkle of fresh or dried dillweed and a little salt. Add a dollop of dairy sour cream, if desired.

Peas

Cook fresh or frozen peas in a small amount of water until crisp-tender; drain. Add a little butter or margarine and snipped, fresh mint leaves.

Potatoes

Bake potatoes at 425° for 50 to 60 minutes or until tender. Slice in half and scoop out inside, leaving shell; mash. Combine mashed potatoes with dairy sour cream, butter or margarine, shredded cheese, and chopped green onions. Add salt and pepper to taste and milk, if necessary, to make the mixture fluffy. Return potato mixture to the shells. Dot with additional butter or margarine; garnish with a sprinkle of additional green onion. Place on a baking sheet and bake in a 425° oven for about 20 to 25 minutes or until thoroughly heated and tops are golden.

Spinach

Cook fresh or frozen spinach as directed; drain well. Add a small amount of whipping cream and prepared horseradish to taste. Heat through. Or, to the drained spinach, add a little butter or margarine and a dash of balsamic or malt vinegar to taste.

The Salad Bowl...

A distinctive salad can be the crowning touch to your meal. With the recipes in this chapter, you now can concoct tempting salads that are eye-appealing as well as taste-bud-pleasing.

Avocado Salad with Tomato Dressing

Boston, Bibb, and butterhead are all names for the same variety of leaf lettuce. It has a soft, buttery, slightly sweet flavor.

Tomato Dressing:

2 tablespoons red wine vinegar
4 teaspoons tomato paste
1 tablespoon lemon juice
½ teaspoon soy sauce
⅛ teaspoon salt
1 green onion, chopped
1 teaspoon snipped fresh basil or
    ¼ teaspoon dried basil, crushed
2 cloves garlic cloves, minced
⅓ cup olive oil

•••

4 cups torn Boston lettuce
1 large ripe avocado, pitted, peeled, and
    sliced
1 medium cucumber, sliced
  Croutons

Tomato Dressing: In a small bowl, whisk the red wine vinegar, tomato paste, lemon juice, soy sauce, and salt until well blended. Add the green onion, basil, and garlic. Whisk in the olive oil.

Divide the lettuce among 4 individual salad plates. Top with avocado and cucumber slices. Spoon some of the Tomato Dressing over each salad and top with a few croutons.

Serves 4

Per serving: 348 calories, 4 g protein, 19 g carbohydrate, 30 g total fat (5 g saturated), 0 mg cholesterol, 342 mg sodium, 715 mg potassium

Summer Salad with Balsamic Vinaigrette

This salad was designed for the summer when tomatoes and avocados are at their best. To make the croutons like those pictured in the photo, brush bread slices with melted butter and sprinkle with garlic salt. Broil until toasted. Use canape cutters to cut the toasted bread into individual shapes.

Balsamic Vinaigrette:

- 3 tablespoons balsamic vinegar
- 2 tablespoons lemon juice
- 2 cloves garlic, minced
- 1 teaspoon Dijon-style mustard
- ⅛ teaspoon salt
- ⅛ teaspoon pepper
- ⅔ cup olive oil

•••

- 8 cups torn romaine or leaf lettuce
- 1 avocado, peeled and chopped
- 1 large tomato, diced
- 2 green onions, chopped
  Garlic croutons (optional)

Balsamic Vinaigrette: In a small bowl, combine the vinegar, lemon juice, garlic, mustard, salt, and pepper. Whisk in the olive oil.

In a large salad bowl combine the chilled lettuce, the avocado, tomato, and green onions. Whisk the vinaigrette and pour desired amount over the salad. Toss to combine. If desired, sprinkle with garlic croutons.

Serves 4 to 6

Per serving: 436 calories, 4 g protein, 11 g carbohydrate, 45 g total fat (6 g saturated), 0 mg cholesterol, 128 mg sodium, 748 mg potassium

Tomato Salad with Goat Cheese

This is a salad for a warm summer evening. Choose thick, meaty tomatoes—perhaps a combination of red and yellow ones for color. If you prefer, serve the whole recipe in a decorative dish, and pass a crusty loaf of French bread to soak up the juices.

3 large tomatoes

Herb Vinaigrette:
2 tablespoons white wine vinegar
2 teaspoons snipped fresh basil
2 teaspoons snipped fresh parsley
1 teaspoon snipped fresh tarragon
1 teaspoon snipped fresh thyme
½ teaspoon Dijon-style mustard
2 cloves garlic, minced
⅛ teaspoon salt
⅛ teaspoon pepper
¼ cup olive oil

●●●

1 to 2 ounces medium-aged goat cheese

●●●

Lettuce leaves
Fresh herb sprigs (optional)

Slice each tomato into 4 thick slices. Place them in a large shallow dish.

Herb Vinaigrette: In a small bowl, combine the vinegar, basil, parsley, tarragon, thyme, mustard, garlic, salt, and pepper. Whisk in the olive oil. Pour the vinaigrette evenly over the tomatoes.

Crumble the goat cheese over the tomato slices. Cover and marinate in the refrigerator for 1 to 2 hours.

To serve, allow the tomatoes to stand at room temperature for 30 minutes before serving. Arrange the lettuce on 6 individual salad plates. Arrange tomatoes on lettuce. Spoon vinaigrette over tomatoes. If desired, garnish with fresh herb sprigs.

Serves 6

Per serving: 124 calories, 3 g protein, 5 g carbohydrate, 11 g total fat (2 g saturated), 5 mg cholesterol, 85 mg sodium, 229 mg potassium

Spinach Apple Salad with Curry Dressing

Sliced red apples contrast with the greens and pecans to make this salad especially attractive. The subtle hint of curry adds a distinctive taste.

Curry Dressing:

  2 tablespoons cider vinegar
  1 teaspoon sugar
  ½ teaspoon curry powder
  ¼ cup olive oil

• • •

  12 cups torn fresh spinach
  1 tart red apple, unpeeled, thinly sliced
  ¼ cup pecan pieces, toasted, if desired

Curry Dressing: In a small bowl, combine the vinegar, sugar, and curry powder. Whisk in the olive oil.

In a large bowl, combine the spinach and apple slices. Pour the dressing over the spinach and apples and toss lightly. Divide among 4 to 6 individual salad plates and sprinkle with pecans.

Serves 4 to 6

Per serving: 232 calories, 5 g protein, 14 g carbohydrate, 19 g total fat (2 g saturated), 0 mg cholesterol, 133 mg sodium, 1,016 mg potassium

Red, White, and Black Bean Salad

This colorful bean salad, featuring three kinds of beans topped with Cilantro-Lime Dressing, can be quickly assembled for a picnic or potluck dinner. If you prefer, prepare the salad up to 24 hours ahead, and chill it in the refrigerator. Add the avocado just before serving.

Cilantro-Lime Dressing:

- 1 teaspoon toasted cumin seed
- ½ teaspoon toasted coriander seed
- 3 tablespoons fresh lime juice
- 2 tablespoons snipped fresh cilantro
- 3 cloves garlic, minced
- ¼ teaspoon black pepper
- ⅛ teaspoon salt
- ⅛ teaspoon ground red pepper
- ⅓ cup olive oil

• • •

- 1 15-ounce can red beans, rinsed and drained
- 1 15½-ounce can great northern beans, rinsed and drained
- 1 15-ounce can black beans, rinsed and drained
- 1 medium red sweet pepper, chopped
- 1 avocado, pitted, peeled, and chopped
- 4 green onions, thinly sliced

Cilantro-Lime Dressing: In a small skillet, cook the cumin and coriander seeds over low heat for 2 to 3 minutes, stirring often, until lightly browned. Cool and crush in a mortar with pestle. In a small bowl, combine cumin and coriander seeds, lime juice, cilantro, garlic, black pepper, salt, and red pepper. Gradually whisk in olive oil.

In a large bowl, combine the red kidney beans, great northern beans, black beans, sweet pepper, avocado, and green onions. Pour the dressing over the salad and stir gently to coat. Cover and refrigerate for 1 to 2 hours before serving. To serve, allow the salad to stand at room temperature for 30 minutes and stir before serving.

Serves 10 to 12

Per serving: 193 calories, 8 g protein, 20 g carbohydrate, 11 g total fat (2 g saturated), 0 mg cholesterol, 266 mg sodium, 445 mg potassium

Oriental Slaw

Napa cabbage, a variety of Chinese cabbage, is the perfect selection for this oriental-flavored salad. It's crunchy and a little sweeter than head cabbage and has a slight zestiness. Napa cabbage is pictured in the photo on the opposite page.

5 cups shredded cabbage
2 carrots, finely shredded (1 cup)
1 medium red onion, halved and very
   thinly sliced

Honey Vinaigrette:
¼ cup rice vinegar
2 teaspoons honey
½ teaspoon salt
¼ teaspoon ground ginger
¼ teaspoon pepper
¼ cup peanut oil

•••

2 tablespoons dry roasted peanuts,
   finely chopped

In a large bowl, combine the cabbage, carrots, and onion.

Honey Vinaigrette: In a small bowl, combine the vinegar, honey, salt, ginger, and pepper. Whisk in the peanut oil.

Pour the dressing over the vegetables and toss to combine. Cover and refrigerate for 30 minutes to 24 hours to allow the flavors to blend and mellow. Before serving, toss the slaw and sprinkle with the chopped peanuts. Serve with a slotted spoon.

Serves 8

Per serving: 101 calories, 2 g protein, 7 g carbohydrate, 8 g total fat (1 g saturated), 0 mg cholesterol, 168 mg sodium, 201 mg potassium

Southwestern Cherry Tomato Salad

Cherry tomatoes, marinated in a dressing of cumin, coriander, chili powder, and cilantro, go well with a Southwestern or Mexican meal.

1 **pound cherry tomatoes, halved**

Cilantro Dressing:
3 **tablespoons snipped fresh cilantro**
1 **tablespoon lemon juice**
2 **garlic cloves, minced**
¼ **teaspoon ground cumin**
¼ **teaspoon chili powder**
⅛ **teaspoon salt**
⅛ **teaspoon ground red pepper**
⅛ **teaspoon black pepper**
3 **tablespoons olive oil**

Place the cherry tomatoes in a large bowl.

Cilantro Dressing: In a small bowl, combine the cilantro, lemon juice, garlic, cumin, chili powder, salt, red pepper, and black pepper. Whisk in the olive oil.

Pour the dressing over the tomatoes and stir gently to coat. Cover and refrigerate for 2 to 8 hours before serving, stirring occasionally.

Serves 6

Per serving: 79 calories, 1 g protein, 4 g carbohydrate, 7 g total fat 1 g saturated), 0 mg cholesterol, 53 mg sodium, 182 mg potassium

Rising Hopes

Freshly baked bread fills a home with an aroma like no other. Here you can choose from a variety of breads, including a traditional French loaf, popular pita pockets, and a special focaccia.

Orange Brioche

Orange Brioche is heavenly served warm from the oven with butter or toasted and topped with honey. It also makes delicious French toast.

1 package active dry yeast
1 tablespoon sugar
¼ cup warm water (105° to 115°)

•••

½ cup butter
2 tablespoons sugar
4 cups unbleached or all-purpose flour
1 teaspoon orange peel, grated
½ cup orange juice
3 eggs, slightly beaten
1 egg white, slightly beaten
1 teaspoon salt

•••

1 egg yolk
1 tablespoon milk

Dissolve the yeast and the 1 tablespoon sugar in the warm water.

In a large bowl, beat the butter until softened. Beat in the 2 tablespoons sugar, 1 cup of the flour, the orange peel, orange juice, eggs, egg white, and salt. Add the yeast mixture and beat well. Stir in the remaining flour with a large wooden spoon until the dough begins to gather and form a ball. Cover the bowl tightly with plastic wrap, and let dough rise in a warm place until it doubles in size (1½ to 2 hours).

Punch the dough down. Cover it with plastic wrap, and refrigerate for 12 to 24 hours.

Punch the dough down again. Press the dough gently into a buttered 2-quart soufflé mold or dish.

Cover with a light towel and let stand in a warm place until it doubles in size (1½ to 2 hours). Combine the egg yolk and milk, and brush it lightly over the top of the bread.

Bake in a 350° oven for 60 to 65 minutes or until a wooden skewer inserted in the center comes out clean. If necessary, cover with foil the last 20 minutes of baking to prevent overbrowning. Remove from dish. Cool on a wire rack.

Makes 1 loaf (24 servings)

Per serving: 132 calories, 3 g protein, 18 g carbohydrate, 5 g total fat (3 g saturated), 46 mg cholesterol, 139 mg sodium, 43 mg potassium

Peanut Butter Loaf

Those who adore peanut butter will love this bread. Toast a slice and top it with your favorite jelly, or use it to make a BLT.

1 cup milk
½ cup peanut butter
¼ cup sugar
½ teaspoon salt

•••

1 package active dry yeast
½ cup warm water (105° to 115°)
4 to 4½ cups unbleached flour or
**   all-purpose flour**

In a small saucepan, heat the milk over medium heat until hot, but not boiling. Pour the milk into a large bowl. Add the peanut butter, sugar, and salt. Blend well with a wire whisk. Let mixture stand until lukewarm (105° to 115°).

Dissolve the yeast in the warm water. Stir dissolved yeast into the milk mixture. Mix in the flour 1 cup at a time until the dough can be handled. Turn the dough out onto a lightly floured surface. Knead in enough remaining flour to make a moderately soft dough that is smooth and elastic (about 3 to 5 minutes). Place the dough in a lightly greased bowl; turn dough once to grease its surface. Cover with a towel, and let the dough rise in a warm place for about 1 hour or until it doubles in size. Punch the dough down, and divide it in half. Cover with a towel and let rest for 10 minutes.

Shape the dough into 2 loaves and place in 2 greased 7½x3½x2-inch loaf pans. Cover and let rise for 30 to 45 minutes or until it nearly doubles in size.

Bake in a 375° oven for about 30 minutes or until the bread sounds hollow when tapped. If necessary, cover with foil the last 20 minutes of baking to prevent overbrowning. Cool bread completely on a wire rack. Store leftover bread in the freezer.

Makes 2 loaves (16 servings each)

*Per serving: 77 calories, 3 g protein, 12 g carbohydrate, 2 g total fat
(1 g saturated), 1 mg cholesterol, 56 mg sodium, 57 mg potassium*

French Bread

Gather a loaf of this fresh, crusty French bread, a bit of cheese, and some wine, and you have a picnic.

2 packages active dry yeast
¼ teaspoon sugar
2 cups warm water (105° to 115°)
5½ to 6 cups unbleached or all-purpose
    flour
2 teaspoons salt
2 tablespoons yellow cornmeal

Dissolve the yeast and sugar in ½ cup of the warm water. Pour the remaining water in a large bowl. Add the yeast mixture, 2 cups of the flour, and the salt and stir until smooth. Gradually stir in as much of the remaining flour as you can.

Turn the dough out onto a lightly floured surface. Knead in enough of the remaining flour to make a stiff dough that is smooth and elastic (about 10 minutes). Shape the dough into a ball. Place the dough in a lightly greased, large bowl; turn dough once to grease its surface. Cover the bowl tightly with plastic wrap. Let dough rise in a warm place about 1 hour or until it doubles in size.

Punch the dough down. Return the dough to the bowl, cover, and let rise for another hour or until it doubles in size.

Punch the dough down again. Divide the dough into 3 equal portions. Roll each portion into a long rope about 2 inches in diameter, tapering the ends. Pinch the seams together.

Lightly oil 3 French bread pans or 2 baking sheets and sprinkle generously with cornmeal. Place each loaf, seam side down, in the pans or on the baking sheets. Cover with a dry towel, and let bread rise in a warm place until it doubles in size (45 to 60 minutes).

Meanwhile, place the oven rack in the center of the oven. Preheat the oven to 425°. When the bread has risen, make 5 diagonal cuts across each loaf with a clean razor blade or very sharp knife. Place the pans or baking sheets in the oven and bake for 20 to 25 minutes or until the loaves are golden brown. For an extra-crisp crust, after placing the bread in the oven, mist it with water from a spray bottle; mist it again after baking for 5 minutes.

Makes 3 loaves (10 servings each)

Per serving: 86 calories, 3 g protein, 18 g carbohydrate, 0 g total fat (0 g saturated), 0 mg cholesterol, 143 mg sodium, 34 mg potassium

White and Rye Pita Bread

Create your own sandwich by stuffing these individual pocket breads with meat, salad, or vegetables. For a party snack, slice pita bread into triangles and serve with a dip.

1 package dry active yeast
⅛ teaspoon sugar
½ cup warm water (105° to 115°)

• • •

3¾ to 4¼ cups unbleached or all-purpose
   flour
¼ cup rye flour
1 teaspoon salt
2 tablespoons olive oil
¾ cup warm water

• • •

Cornmeal

Dissolve the yeast and sugar in the ½ cup of warm water. In a large bowl, combine 3¾ cups of the all-purpose flour, the rye flour, and salt. Stir in the dissolved yeast and olive oil. Slowly stir in the ¾ cup of warm water until the dough can be formed into a ball.

Turn the dough out onto a lightly floured surface. Knead in enough of the remaining flour to make a dough that is smooth and elastic (about 10 minutes). Place the dough in a lightly greased bowl; turn dough once to grease its surface. Cover the bowl tightly with plastic wrap. Let the dough rise in a warm place about 1 hour or until it doubles in size.

Punch the dough down. Shape it into 8 balls, each 3 inches in diameter. Place them on a lightly floured surface and cover with a clean towel. Let rest for 10 minutes. (If necessary for easier rolling, let dough rest a little longer.) On a lightly floured surface, roll the balls into rounds about 6 to 8 inches in diameter and ⅛ inch thick. Place the rounds on 3 greased baking sheets sprinkled with cornmeal. Place an oven rack in the center of the oven and another rack in the lowest position. Preheat the oven to 500°.

Bake the pita bread, 1 baking sheet at a time, on the bottom rack for 5 minutes. Move to the center rack and bake for about 3 minutes more or until the bread begins to turn golden. (Or, use just center shelf and preheat prepared baking sheets in 500° oven for 1 minute. Place dough rounds on hot baking sheets and bake 8 minutes or until golden.)

Remove from the oven; immediately wrap individually in aluminum foil and let stand for 10 minutes. This helps form the pocket in the bread. Remove pita pockets from the foil, and let them cool on a baking rack. For softer bread, place them in an open plastic bag until completely cooled.

Makes 8 pita pockets

Per serving: 257 calories, 7 g protein, 48 g carbohydrate, 4 g total fat (1 g saturated), 0 mg cholesterol, 268 mg sodium, 91 mg potassium

Focaccia

Focaccia is an Italian country-style flat bread. This version is topped with caramelized onion, cheese, pine nuts, and garlic. Serve it with a salad, a pasta dish, or as an appetizer.

3 to 3½ cups unbleached or all-purpose flour
1 package active dry yeast
1⅓ cups warm water (120° to 130°)
¼ teaspoon sugar
1 tablespoon olive oil
1 teaspoon salt
½ cup stone ground rye flour

•••

4 tablespoons olive oil
1 large onion, thinly sliced
2 large cloves garlic, peeled and thinly sliced
2 tablespoons pine nuts
¼ teaspoon coarse salt
½ cup grated Romano or Parmesan cheese

In a large mixing bowl, combine 1½ cups of the unbleached flour, the yeast, water, sugar, 1 tablespoon olive oil, and salt. Beat with an electric mixer on low speed for 30 seconds, scraping the bowl. Beat on high speed for 3 minutes. Stir in rye flour and as much of the remaining unbleached flour as you can.

Turn the dough out onto a lightly floured surface. Knead in enough of the remaining flour to make a moderately stiff dough that is smooth and elastic (6 to 8 minutes). Place the dough in a lightly greased bowl; turn dough once to grease surface. Cover bowl tightly with plastic wrap. Let dough rise in a warm place for about 1 hour or until it doubles in size.

Punch the dough down, and divide it in half. Cover and let rest for 10 minutes.

Meanwhile, cook onions in 2 tablespoons of the olive oil in a large skillet over low heat for about 10 minutes or until tender; set aside.

On a lightly floured surface, roll or shape each half of the dough into a 12-inch round about ¼ inch thick. Place each round on a lightly greased 12-inch pizza pan.

Press half of the sliced garlic and half of the pine nuts deeply into each round. Spread half of the cooked onion mixture on top of each round and press in. Cover with a towel and let rise for 30 minutes.

Lightly sprinkle each round with coarse salt and half of the grated cheese. Drizzle 1 tablespoon of the remaining olive oil over the top of each round. Bake in a 400° oven for 15 to 20 minutes or until the bread is lightly browned.

Makes two 12-inch rounds (8 servings each)

Per serving: 156 calories, 4 g protein, 22 g carbohydrate, 6 g total fat (0 g saturated), 0 mg cholesterol, 0 mg sodium, 0 mg potassium

Canning and Condiments...........

Pungent relishes for canning
and savory sauces for freezing
fill this chapter. Many of these
sensational recipes let you
make good use of a bountiful
tomato harvest.

Dilled Green Tomatoes

Small, unripened tomatoes are great for pickling. Serve this spicy treat on a salad or as part of a condiment tray.

3 pounds small unripened (green)
    cherry tomatoes
16 dried red chili peppers
16 cloves garlic, peeled
8 to 16 sprigs fresh dillweed

•••

4 cups white vinegar
4 cups distilled water
6 tablespoons pickling salt

Rinse and stem the tomatoes and set aside. Sterilize six 1-pint wide-mouth canning jars and lids. Place 2 red chili peppers, 2 cloves garlic, and 1 to 2 dill sprigs in each jar. Pack the tomatoes tightly in the jars.

In a large pan, bring the vinegar, water, and salt to boiling. Pour over the tomatoes, leaving a ¼-inch headspace. Wipe jars, adjust lids, and process in a boiling-water bath for 15 minutes.

Makes 8 pints

Per ¼-cup serving: 13 calories, 1 g protein, 2 g carbohydrate, 0 g total fat (0 g saturated), 0 mg cholesterol, 604 mg sodium, 86 mg potassium

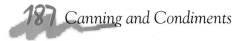

Spicy Tomato Sauce with Roasted Peppers

Colorful and flavorful, this sauce makes a good topping for Boboli (an Italian bread shell). Just heat the sauce, spread it over the shell, and top with Parmesan cheese and basil leaves.

5 large or 7 medium sweet peppers
   (green, red, yellow, and/or orange),
   or 2 cups purchased roasted red
   peppers

• • •

4 pounds Italian plum tomatoes

• • •

2 tablespoons olive oil
1 cup finely chopped onion,
6 cloves garlic, finely chopped

• • •

3 tablespoons snipped fresh basil
1 teaspoon sugar
1 teaspoon salt
½ teaspoon crushed red pepper

Cut the peppers in half and remove the stems, seeds, and membranes. Place them on a foil-lined baking sheet, cut sides down. Place baking sheets under the oven broiler for 3 to 5 minutes or until the peppers are wrinkled and charred. (Or, place the baking sheet with the peppers in a 425° oven for about 20 minutes.) Place the peppers in a sealed paper bag for 20 minutes to steam for easier peeling. Peel the roasted peppers. Slice them into ⅜-inch strips about 2 inches long; set aside. (You should have about 2 cups.)

To prepare the tomatoes, slice an X with a sharp knife through the skin at the base of each tomato. Place the tomatoes, a few at a time, in a pot of boiling water until the skins begin to wrinkle (about 30 seconds). Remove them from the pot, and immediately plunge them into a pan of ice water. Cool for several minutes. Remove and discard the skins and cores. Chop the tomatoes into small pieces. (You should have 6 cups.)

Heat the olive oil in a large saucepan or Dutch oven over medium-low heat. Add the onion and garlic and cook, stirring frequently, for 5 minutes or until the onions are tender. Stir in the tomatoes, peppers, basil, sugar, salt, and crushed red pepper. Bring to boiling; reduce heat. Boil gently, uncovered, for 25 minutes or until sauce is thickened to desired consistency. Taste and adjust seasonings, if desired; cool.

To freeze, cool mixture quickly by setting pan into a sink of ice water. Pour the sauce into freezer containers or bags. Seal, label, and freeze.

Makes about 5 cups

Per ½-cup serving: 95 calories, 3 g protein, 16 g carbohydrate, 4 g total fat (1 g saturated), 0 mg cholesterol, 232 mg sodium, 588 mg potassium

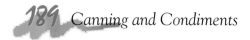

Tomato Sauce with Garlic, Basil, and Olives

The hearty trio of garlic, basil, and olives give texture and dimension to this tomato sauce. Serve it over your favorite pasta.

8 pounds plum tomatoes

•••

½ **cup olive oil**
¼ **cup finely chopped garlic**
⅓ **cup snipped fresh basil**
1 **teaspoon salt**
½ **teaspoon pepper**
½ **cup pitted ripe olives, sliced**
½ **cup pimento-stuffed green olives,**
   sliced

To prepare the tomatoes, slice an X with a sharp knife through the skin at the base of each tomato. Place the tomatoes, a few at a time, in a pot of boiling water until the skins begin to wrinkle (about 30 seconds). Remove them from the pot, and immediately plunge them into a pan of ice water. Cool for several minutes. Remove and discard the skins and cores. Chop the tomatoes into small pieces. (You should have 12 cups.)

Heat the olive oil in a large saucepan or Dutch oven over medium heat. Add the garlic. Cook for about 5 minutes, stirring gently, until the garlic begins to turn golden. Watch closely to prevent it from burning. Add the tomatoes, basil, salt, and pepper. Bring to boiling; reduce the heat. Boil gently for 10 minutes, stirring occasionally. Stir in the olives and cook 2 minutes more. Taste and adjust seasonings, if desired; cool.

To freeze, cool mixture quickly by setting pan into a sink of ice water. Pour the sauce into freezer containers or bags. Seal, label, and freeze.

Makes 6 pints

Per ½-cup serving: 84 calories, 2 g protein, 9 g carbohydrate, 6 g total fat (1 g saturated), 0 mg cholesterol, 196 mg sodium, 361 mg potassium

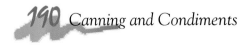

Last Chance Tomato Sauce

As fall's first frost approaches, gather the last of the garden tomatoes to make a batch of this zesty sauce. Freezing it makes the task a simple one.

7 to 8 pounds fresh tomatoes

•••

¼ cup olive oil
1½ cups chopped onion
1 cup chopped green sweet pepper
1 cup chopped yellow or orange sweet pepper
6 cloves garlic, finely chopped
2 tablespoons snipped fresh basil or 1 teaspoon dried basil, crushed
1½ teaspoons dried oregano, crushed
¼ teaspoon dried tarragon, crushed
½ to 1 teaspoon crushed red pepper
1 tablespoon sugar
1½ teaspoons salt
¼ teaspoon pepper

To prepare the tomatoes, slice an X with a sharp knife through the skin at the base of each tomato. Place the tomatoes, a few at a time, in a pot of boiling water until the skins begin to wrinkle (about 30 seconds). Remove them from the pot, and immediately plunge them into a pan of ice water. Cool for several minutes. Remove and discard the skins and cores. Chop the tomatoes into small pieces. (You should have 12 cups.)

Heat the olive oil in a large saucepan or Dutch oven over low heat. Add the onion, peppers, and garlic and cook until tender, stirring occasionally. Add the tomatoes, basil, oregano, tarragon, crushed red pepper, sugar, salt, and pepper. Simmer, uncovered, over low heat, stirring occasionally, for about 2 hours or until the sauce thickens slightly. Taste and adjust seasonings, if desired; cool.

To freeze, cool mixture quickly by setting pan into a sink of ice water. Pour the sauce into freezer containers or bags. Seal, label, and freeze.

Makes 4 pints

Per ½-cup serving: 66 calories, 2 g protein, 11 g carbohydrate, 3 g total fat (0 g saturated), 0 mg cholesterol, 124 mg sodium, 435 mg potassium

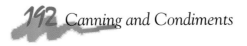

Hot Pickled Okra

This pickled okra is hot with a crisp texture. Serve it with sandwiches or as a party snack. If you have hard tap water, use distilled water instead. It will make the pickled okra less cloudy.

2 pounds fresh okra
12 cloves garlic, unpeeled
12 dried red chili peppers

•••

4 cups cider vinegar
4 cups water
6 tablespoons pickling salt

Rinse the okra and set aside. Sterilize six 1-pint wide-mouth canning jars and lids. Place 2 cloves garlic and 2 dried red chili peppers in each jar. Pack the okra tightly in the jars.

In a large saucepan, bring the vinegar, water, and salt to boiling. Pour over the okra, leaving a ½-inch headspace. Wipe jars, adjust lids, and process in a boiling-water bath for 10 minutes. Store at least 1 month before opening.

Makes 6 pints

Per ¼-cup serving: 15 calories, 1 g protein, 4 g carbohydrate, 0 g total fat (0 g saturated), 0 mg cholesterol, 801 mg sodium, 122 mg potassium

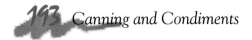

Pickled Sweet Banana Peppers

Try these spicy peppers on sandwiches or salads when you want a piquant flavor without too much heat. (Dilled Green Tomatoes, page 187, and Hot Pickled Okra, page 193, are also pictured at left.)

2 pounds sweet banana peppers
3 dried red chili peppers
3 cloves garlic, peeled

•••

2 cups cider vinegar
2 cups water
2 tablespoons pickling salt

Rinse the peppers and cut off the tops. Slice lengthwise down one side of each pepper and remove seeds and membranes. Slice pepper crosswise into rings about ¼-inch wide. Sterilize three 1-pint wide-mouth canning jars and lids. Place 1 dried red chili and 1 clove garlic in each jar. Pack the pepper rings tightly in the jars.

In a large pan, bring the vinegar, water, and pickling salt to boiling. Pour over the pepper rings, leaving a ¼-inch headspace. Wipe jars, adjust lids, and process in a boiling water bath for 10 minutes.

Makes 3 pints

Per ¼-cup serving: 21 calories, 1 g protein, 5 g carbohydrate, 0 g total fat (0 g saturated), 0 mg cholesterol, 536 mg sodium, 169 mg potassium

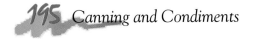

Tomato Salsa

Salsa is a favorite at every party—and this one is so easy to make from scratch! The flavor has a pleasant blend of sweetness and hotness. Whenever you work with hot peppers, be sure to protect yourself by covering one or both hands with plastic bags (or plastic gloves). Be sure to wash your hands thoroughly before touching your eyes or face.

4½ **pounds fresh tomatoes**

•••

2 **tablespoons olive oil**
1½ **cups chopped yellow onions**
2 **jalapeño peppers, seeded and chopped**

•••

4 **garlic cloves, chopped**
2 to 3 **tablespoons sugar**
1 **teaspoon dried oregano, crushed**
¾ **teaspoon salt**
½ **teaspoon pepper**

To prepare the tomatoes, slice an X with a sharp knife through the skin at the base of each tomato. Place the tomatoes, a few at a time, in a pot of boiling water until the skins begin to wrinkle (about 30 seconds). Remove them from the pot, and immediately plunge them into a pan of ice water. Cool for several minutes. Remove and discard the skins and cores. Chop the tomatoes into small pieces. (You should have 8 cups.)

Heat the olive oil in a 6-quart Dutch oven over medium-low heat. Add the chopped onion and jalapeño peppers. Cook slowly until the onion is very tender. Add the tomatoes, garlic, sugar, oregano, salt, and pepper. Bring to boiling; reduce heat. Simmer, uncovered, over low heat, stirring occasionally, for about 1 hour or until the salsa reduces and thickens slightly; cool.

Pour the salsa into jars or freezer containers or bags. Seal, label, and store in the refrigerator or freezer.

Makes 4½ cups

Per tablespoon: 11 calories, 0 g protein, 2 g carbohydrate, 1 g total fat (0 g saturated), 0 mg cholesterol, 28 mg sodium, 70 mg potassium

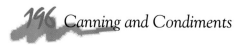

Red Chili Salsa

Plenty of garlic flavor is packed into this special salsa. Serve it traditionally with corn chips or use it as a base for chili.

12 **large whole garlic cloves, unpeeled**

•••

8 **pounds fresh tomatoes**

•••

3 **tablespoons red wine vinegar**
1 **teaspoon dried oregano, crushed**
1½ **teaspoons crushed red pepper**
2 to 3 **tablespoons sugar**
1 to 1½ **teaspoons salt**

•••

4 **cloves garlic, minced**

Place the unpeeled cloves garlic on a piece of aluminum foil. Sprinkle with a few drops of water and seal the foil tightly around the garlic. Bake in a 375° oven about 45 minutes or until the garlic is very tender. Press the garlic to extract the puree.

To prepare the tomatoes, slice an X with a sharp knife through the skin at the base of each tomato. Place the tomatoes, a few at a time, in a pot of boiling water until the skins begin to wrinkle (about 30 seconds). Remove them from the pot, and immediately plunge them into a pan of ice water. Cool for several minutes. Remove and discard the skins and cores. Chop the tomatoes into small pieces. (You should have 12 cups.)

Place the tomatoes in a large pan or Dutch oven. Add the garlic puree, vinegar, oregano, crushed red pepper, sugar, and salt. Simmer the salsa, uncovered, over low heat, stirring occasionally, for 45 minutes. Add the minced garlic and cook for 30 minutes more. Season to taste; cool. Serve the salsa as is, or, for a smoother version, puree it in a blender or food processor.

Pour the salsa into jars or freezer containers or bags. Seal, label, and store in the refrigerator or freezer.

Makes 8 cups

Per tablespoon: 7 calories, 0 g protein, 2 g carbohydrate, 0 g total fat (0 g saturated), 0 mg cholesterol, 19 mg sodium, 65 mg potassium

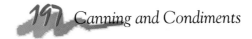

Marinated Sweet Peppers

This versatile condiment adds color and flavor to an antipasto tray, salads, sandwiches, grilled fish, or pasta dishes.

2 pounds mixed sweet peppers (red, yellow, orange, and/or green)

Marinade:
1 tablespoon white wine vinegar
2 cloves garlic, minced
¼ teaspoon salt
3 tablespoons olive oil

Cut the peppers in half and remove the stems, seeds, and membranes. Place them on a foil-lined baking sheet, cut sides down. Place baking sheets under the oven broiler for 3 to 5 minutes or until the peppers are wrinkled and charred. (Or, place the baking sheet with the peppers in a 425° oven for about 20 minutes.) Place the peppers in a sealed paper bag for 20 minutes to steam for easier peeling.

Peel the peppers. Cut them into strips ½-inch wide. Place them in a refrigerator container.

Marinade: In a small bowl, combine the vinegar, garlic, and salt. Whisk in the olive oil.

Pour the marinade over pepper strips. Cover the container with a tight lid, and turn container to coat the peppers. Refrigerate for at least 24 hours before using, stirring occasionally. Store in the refrigerator for up to 3 weeks.

Makes 1 pint

Per ¼-cup serving: 77 calories, 1 g protein, 8 g carbohydrate, 5 g total fat (1 g saturated), 0 mg cholesterol, 70 mg sodium, 217 mg potassium

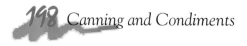

Ma Steeves' Sweet Mustard

This hot mustard is excellent served with baked ham or roast beef sandwiches, and it makes a great food gift.

1 2-ounce can dry mustard
1 cup white vinegar

•••

2 eggs, well beaten
1 cup sugar
1 teaspoon salt

Combine the mustard and vinegar. Cover and let stand unrefrigerated overnight.

Combine the eggs, sugar, and salt in a medium saucepan. Add the mustard and vinegar mixture and mix well. Cook over medium heat, stirring constantly, until mixture starts to thicken and bubble. Do not boil. Reduce the heat. Cook and stir for 1 minute more.

Strain the mustard and pour into jars or storage containers. Cool to room temperature, cover, and refrigerate. The mustard will thicken further after refrigeration.

Makes about 1½ cups

Per tablespoon: 51 calories, 1 g protein, 8 g carbohydrate, 0 g total fat (0 g saturated), 18 mg cholesterol, 95 mg sodium, 17 mg potassium

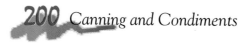

Sweet Dreams

A fitting finale to any fine meal is a sweet treat. Here you'll find traditional favorites with a flair and festive specialty items for entertaining.

Key Lime Tart with Raspberry Puree

A simple sauce of pureed raspberries pairs well with this creamy lime pie. When buying whipping cream for the filling, choose one that has at least 36 percent milk fat so the tart sets up firmly. In some areas, it may be called heavy whipping cream or heavy cream.

Pastry:

- ½ cup butter, softened
- ¼ cup sugar
- ¼ teaspoon salt
- 1 egg
- ½ teaspoon almond extract
- 1½ cups all-purpose flour

Key Lime Filling:

- 4 egg yolks
- 1 teaspoon grated lime peel
- ¼ cup Key lime juice
- 1 cup sugar
- ⅛ teaspoon salt
- 2 tablespoons butter
- 1 cup whipping cream

Raspberry Puree:

- 1 10 ounce package of frozen red raspberries in syrup, thawed

•••

- **Fresh raspberries (optional)**

Pastry: Using an electric mixer, cream the ½ cup butter until fluffy. Add the ¼ cup sugar and ¼ teaspoon salt and mix well. Beat in egg and almond extract. Add the flour gradually, mixing just until combined. Shape the dough into a ball, and wrap it in waxed paper. Chill for 1 hour. On a lightly floured surface, roll out the dough to fit a 10-inch tart pan with a removable bottom. Press dough firmly and evenly into the pan and prick with a fork. Bake in a 425° oven for 8 to 10 minutes.

Key Lime Filling: Place the egg yolks in a small bowl. Beat lightly and set aside. In the top of a double boiler over low heat, combine the lime peel, lime juice, 1 cup sugar, ⅛ teaspoon salt, and 2 tablespoons butter. Stir occasionally until the butter melts and the sugar is dissolved. Remove the pan from heat. Add some of the lime mixture, 1 tablespoon at a time, to the egg yolks, stirring constantly. Slowly pour the egg mixture into the lime mixture, stirring constantly. Return the pan to the heat and cook, stirring constantly, until the mixture thickens and coats the back of the spoon (12 to 15 minutes). (The water in the bottom of the double boiler should simmer, not boil, or filling may curdle.) Pour the filling into a large bowl and cool slightly.

Meanwhile, whip the cream until stiff peaks form. Gently fold the whipped cream into the lime filling. Pour the filling into the tart shell. Chill for 6 to 24 hours before serving.

Raspberry Puree. In a blender container or food processor bowl, blend or process the raspberries (with syrup) until smooth. Pour through a wire mesh strainer to strain the seeds. If made ahead, store puree in refrigerator, and allow it to return to room temperature before serving.

To serve, spoon the puree onto dessert plates, top with tart wedges. Or, spoon puree over tart wedges. If desired, garnish with fresh raspberries.

Serves 8

Per serving: 478 calories, 5 g protein, 51 g carbohydrate, 29 g total fat (17 g saturated), 213 mg cholesterol, 154 mg sodium, 69 mg potassium

Perfect Pecan Pie

This is a not-so-sweet version of everyone's favorite.

4 eggs
1 cup light corn syrup
½ cup packed brown sugar
¼ cup butter or margarine, melted
1 teaspoon vanilla
1 cup pecan halves

•••

1 9-inch unbaked pastry shell

For filling, in a mixing bowl, beat eggs lightly with a rotary beater or fork until combined. Add corn syrup, sugar, butter or margarine, and vanilla; stir well. Stir in pecan halves.

Pour the filling into the pastry shell. Bake in a 350° oven for 40 to 45 minutes or until a knife inserted near the center comes out clean.

Cool pie on a wire rack. Serve warm or cover and chill to store.

Serves 8 to 10

Per serving: 456 calories, 6 g protein, 54 g carbohydrate, 26 g total fat (7 g saturated), 122 mg cholesterol, 208 mg sodium, 108 mg potassium

Coconut Flan

This simple flan is made with coconut milk and topped with a caramelized sugar topping. Garnish it with tropical fruits.

1 cup unsweetened coconut milk
1 cup half-and-half or light cream
½ cup sugar
6 egg yolks

•••

⅓ cup sugar

Combine the coconut milk, half-and-half or light cream, and the ¼ cup sugar in a saucepan. Scald the mixture over medium-high heat. Remove from heat. Place the egg yolks in a large bowl and beat lightly. Gradually add the hot milk mixture, stirring constantly with a wire whip. (Add milk very slowly or the eggs will curdle.) Strain, if desired, and set aside.

Melt the ⅓ cup of sugar over low heat in a small, heavy skillet. Stir occasionally until it turns a deep golden brown. Immediately pour a small amount of the caramelized sugar into six 6-ounce custard cups.

Place the custard cups in a large shallow baking dish. Pour the egg-and-milk mixture into the custard cups. Place the baking dish in the oven and add about 1 inch of boiling water to the dish. Cover the baking dish tightly with aluminum foil and bake in a 350° oven for 20 to 30 minutes or until the flan is set (knife comes out clean).

Remove the custard cups from baking dish and cool. Cover and refrigerate for 4 to 24 hours. To serve, run a knife around the edges of the custard cups and invert them onto dessert plates.

Serves 6

Per serving: 278 calories, 5 g protein, 24 g carbohydrate, 19 g total fat (13 g saturated), 228 mg cholesterol, 30 mg sodium, 174 mg potassium

 Raspberry Mousse Pie

For those who like crust under their mousse, this dessert is the perfect treat. Fresh raspberries and mint leaves lend brilliant color as a garnish.

1½ **teaspoons unflavored gelatin**
3 **tablespoons cold water**

•••

1 **10-ounce carton frozen red**
   raspberries in heavy syrup, thawed
1 **cup whipping cream**
3 **tablespoons sugar**
½ **teaspoon vanilla**

•••

1 **9-inch pie shell, baked and cooled**

Place the gelatin in a small saucepan. Pour the cold water over the gelatin and stir. Let stand 5 minutes. Place over low heat; cook and stir until gelatin is completely dissolved.

Place the raspberries in a medium bowl. Stir the gelatin mixture into the raspberries. If necessary, refrigerate until mixture is partially set (consistency of egg whites). The time needed will depend on the temperature of the raspberries. Do not allow the mixture to become completely firm.

Whip the cream until it begins to thicken. Add the sugar and vanilla and continue whipping until soft peaks form. Fold the raspberry mixture into the cream. Pour into a pie shell, cover, and chill for 3 to 24 hours before serving.

Serves 8 to 10

Per serving: 277 calories, 3 g protein, 26 g carbohydrate, 19 g total fat (9 g saturated), 41 mg cholesterol, 134 mg sodium, 78 mg potassium

Crepes with Crème Patisserie

Prepare this French speciality for your holiday party. To save time, the crème patisserie and crepes can be made the day before and refrigerated until you're ready to assemble this delightful dessert.

Crème Patisserie:

1½ cups milk
3 egg yolks
⅔ cup sugar
½ cup all-purpose flour

•••

1 tablespoon butter or margarine
4 teaspoons rum
1½ teaspoons vanilla

Crepes:

3 eggs
⅔ cup all-purpose flour
1 cup milk

•••

Melted butter or margarine

•••

½ cup semisweet chocolate pieces
Powdered sugar

Crème Patisserie: In a small pan, heat milk almost to boiling; set aside. In a large bowl, using a large wire whip, beat the egg yolks and sugar together until mixture is pale yellow and forms a ribbon. Beat in the flour until smooth. Slowly pour in the hot milk in a thin stream, beating constantly.

Pour the mixture into a heavy 1½-quart saucepan. Stir over medium-high heat using a wire whip. The custard will become lumpy as it nears the boiling point, but will smooth out as you continue to stir. When it starts to boil, reduce heat to low and stir for 2 to 3 minutes more.

Remove from the heat and add the butter or margarine, rum, and vanilla. Cover surface with plastic wrap. Cool about 1 hour.

Crepes: In a blender container or food processor bowl, blend or process the eggs and flour. While machine is running, slowly add the milk, blending until smooth. Place a 6- or 7-inch frying pan over medium heat. When hot, brush the pan with small amount of melted butter or margarine. Pour in about 2 tablespoons of the crepe batter, tilting the pan so the batter flows quickly over its entire surface. Cook just until the edges are lightly browned and surface looks dry. Using a wide spatula, carefully turn the crepe over and brown lightly on the other side. Turn the cooked crepes onto a flat surface to cool.

To assemble, if desired, fill a pastry bag with Crème Patisserie. Pipe or spoon about 2 tablespoons filling just below the center of each crepe. Fold each crepe in half and fold again to form a triangle.

Melt the chocolate pieces in a small heavy saucepan over low heat. Dip the tip of each crepe triangle in the melted chocolate. Cool slightly. Arrange on a large platter and sprinkle with powdered sugar.

Serves 8

Per serving: 289 calories, 8 g protein, 41 g carbohydrate, 10 g total fat (5 g saturated), 169 mg cholesterol, 80 mg sodium, 183 mg potassium

Chestnut Soufflé with Grand Marnier Cream

Serve this soufflé with champagne for a festive finish to a holiday dinner.

½ cup chestnut puree
1 cup milk

•••

3 tablespoons butter or margarine
3 tablespoons all-purpose flour

•••

¼ cup sugar
1 tablespoon finely shredded orange
 peel
6 egg yolks
6 egg whites

Grand Marnier Cream:
1 cup whipping cream
2 tablespoons sugar
1 teaspoon grated orange peel
2 to 4 tablespoons Grand Marnier or
 other orange liqueur

Spoon chestnut puree into a small saucepan. Gradually stir in milk until smooth. Bring just to boiling over medium heat.

Meanwhile, in a medium saucepan, melt the butter or margarine over medium heat. Add the flour, stirring for 2 minutes. Remove the pan from the heat, and slowly add the boiling milk mixture, beating with a wire whip until blended.

Return the mixture to the heat and cook for 1 minute. It should be very thick. Remove from heat, and add the sugar and orange peel. Gradually add the mixture to the egg yolks, stirring until well blended.

Using an electric mixer, beat the egg whites in a large bowl until stiff peaks form. Stir some of the beaten egg whites into the egg yolk mixture to lighten it. Carefully fold the egg yolk-egg white mixture into the remaining beaten egg whites.

Pour the mixture into a buttered 2½-quart soufflé dish. Bake in a 375° oven about 30 minutes. The soufflé should be firm around the edges and slightly soft in the center when it is done.

Grand Marnier Cream: Whip the cream until thick but not stiff. Beat in the sugar, orange peel, and liqueur just until combined.

To serve, cut the soufflé with two large serving spoons and place in serving bowls. Top each with a dollop of Grand Marnier Cream.

Serves 8 to 10

Per serving: 301 calories, 7 g protein, 22 g carbohydrate, 20 g total fat (11 g saturated), 214 mg cholesterol, 116 mg sodium, 192 mg potassium

Gâteau au Chocolat

This rich chocolate cake is the perfect ending to an elegant dinner party. It is very easy to make and can be prepared a day or two ahead. Since it is extremely rich, serve petite slices to your guests along with strong espresso coffee.

1 cup butter
6 ounces milk chocolate pieces (1 cup)
3 ounces unsweetened chocolate, cut up

•••

4 eggs
1¼ cups sugar
1 tablespoon all-purpose flour
1 teaspoon vanilla
1 cup coarsely chopped walnuts

Chocolate Glaze:

¼ cup butter
2 ounces semisweet chocolate, cut up,
    or ⅓ cup semisweet chocolate pieces
2 ounces unsweetened chocolate, cut up
2 teaspoons light corn syrup
12 to 16 walnut halves

Butter the bottom and 1 inch up the sides of a 9-inch springform pan. Wrap a 12-inch square-piece of aluminum foil around the bottom and up the outside of the pan. Set aside.

In a heavy saucepan, combine the butter, milk chocolate pieces, and unsweetened chocolate. Cook over low heat, stirring constantly, until chocolate is melted.

In a large bowl, beat the eggs with a wire whip. Whisk in the sugar and flour. Add the vanilla. Slowly pour in the chocolate mixture, stirring to combine. Stir in the chopped walnuts. Pour the mixture into the springform pan. Place the springform pan in a large baking pan. Pour boiling water to a depth of ½ inch into the baking pan.

Bake in a 325° oven about 1 hour or until a toothpick inserted near the center comes out with only a few moist crumbs attached. Remove the springform pan from the water and cool completely on a wire rack. When ready to glaze, loosen, release, and carefully remove the pan sides.

Chocolate Glaze: In a heavy saucepan, combine the butter, semisweet chocolate, unsweetened chocolate, and corn syrup. Cook over low heat, stirring constantly, until chocolate is melted. Remove the pan from the heat; cool to room temperature, stirring occasionally. Beat with a wire whip until mixture thickens slightly. Pour the glaze over the cake and smooth carefully with a metal spatula. Quickly decorate the top of the cake with walnut halves. After the glaze has set, cover and refrigerate until ready to serve. Remove from the refrigerator about 15 minutes before serving.

Serves 12 to 16

Per serving: 501 calories, 7 g protein, 38 g carbohydrate, 39 g total fat (20 g saturated), 126 mg cholesterol, 232 mg sodium, 232 mg potassium

Rose Petal Cake

This delightful floral cake will have your guests wondering what that mysterious, but delicious, flavor is. Let them guess! For a clue, decorate the cake with candied rose petals.

2¼ cups sifted cake flour
1½ cups sugar
  3 teaspoons baking powder
  ½ teaspoon salt
  ½ cup cooking oil
  5 egg yolks
  ¾ cup water
  3 to 4 teaspoons rose water

•••

  1 cup egg whites (6 or 7 large eggs)
  ½ teaspoon cream of tartar

Glaze:
  1 cup powdered sugar
  3 to 4 tablespoons half-and-half or
     light cream
  ¼ teaspoon rose water
  1 or 2 drops red food coloring

Sift the flour, sugar, baking powder, and salt together into a very large mixing bowl. Make a well in the dry ingredients. Add, in order, the oil, egg yolks, water, and 3 to 4 teaspoons rose water, beating with a mixer after each addition until smooth.

Wash beaters. Using an electric mixer, beat the egg whites with the cream of tartar in a large bowl until very stiff peaks form. Pour the batter slowly into the beaten egg whites, folding gently with a large spoon. Pour the batter into an ungreased 10-inch tube pan.

Bake in a 350° oven for 1 hour. Invert the pan to cool. Remove the cake from the pan when completely cool.

Glaze: With a wire whip, combine the powdered sugar, half-and-half or light cream, and ¼ teaspoon rose water; beat until smooth and of drizzling consistency. Stir in red food coloring to produce a pleasing shade of pale pink. Slowly pour the glaze over the cake, letting it run down the sides.

Serves 10

Per serving: 376 calories, 5 g protein, 58 g carbohydrate, 14 g total fat (2 g saturated), 108 mg cholesterol, 238 mg sodium, 92 mg potassium

Fresh Peaches with Lemon Yogurt Cheese

For a light and easy dessert, serve fresh peaches topped with lemon yogurt cheese on a pool of raspberry puree.

Yogurt Cheese:

1 8-ounce carton lemon-flavor or peach-flavor low-fat yogurt (without gelatin added)
1 tablespoon powdered sugar

•••

1 10-ounce carton frozen red raspberries in syrup, thawed
2 large fresh peaches or nectarines

Yogurt Cheese: Place a medium-size wire-mesh strainer over a medium bowl. Line the strainer with several thicknesses of 100% cotton cheesecloth. Spoon the yogurt into the cheesecloth. Place in the refrigerator for 12 to 24 hours to drain the liquids from the yogurt. Then, carefully turn the yogurt over onto a new piece of cheesecloth, return it to the strainer, and refrigerate for at least 12 hours more to allow it to drain from the other side. (It will be somewhat firm.) Place the yogurt cheese in a small bowl. Add the powdered sugar and stir to combine. Cover and refrigerate until ready to serve.

In a blender container or food processor bowl, blend or process the raspberries (with syrup) until smooth. Pour through a wire-mesh strainer to remove the seeds. Store the puree in the refrigerator until ready to serve.

To serve, peel the peaches, if desired. Cut each peach or nectarine in half lengthwise and remove the pit. Slice each half into thin slices. Pour a small amount of the raspberry puree in the center of 4 dessert plates. Arrange the peaches or nectarines on the puree. Top each with a large dollop of lemon yogurt cheese.

Serves 4

Per serving: 114 calories, 3 g protein, 25 g carbohydrate, 1 g total fat (0 g saturated), 2 mg cholesterol, 33 mg sodium, 298 mg potassium

Banana Nut Bread

Moist and rich describes this version of banana bread. Serve it plain, or with a scoop of chocolate or vanilla ice cream. For a breakfast treat, toast it and serve it topped with butter and garnished with fresh strawberries.

½ cup butter or margarine, softened
1 cup sugar
2 eggs
1 teaspoon vanilla
1 cup mashed very ripe bananas
    (3 medium bananas)
2 cups all-purpose flour
2 teaspoons baking powder
½ teaspoon baking soda
¼ teaspoon salt
¼ teaspoon ground nutmeg
⅓ cup buttermilk
½ cup chopped pecans

Cream the butter or margarine and sugar. Add the eggs and vanilla and mix well. Add the mashed banana and mix well. In a separate bowl, combine the flour, baking powder, baking soda, salt, and nutmeg. Alternately add the dry ingredients and the buttermilk to the creamed mixture, mixing at low speed just until combined. Stir in the pecans.

Pour the mixture into a greased and floured 9x5x3-inch loaf pan. Bake in a 350° oven for 55 to 60 minutes or until the bread springs back when touched and a wooden toothpick inserted near the center comes out clean. Let cool for 5 to 10 minutes in pan. Remove bread from pan and cool on a wire rack. For easier slicing, wrap and store overnight before serving.

Makes 1 loaf (16 servings)

Per serving: 212 calories, 3 g protein, 31 g carbohydrate, 9 g total fat (4 g saturated), 42 mg cholesterol, 171 mg sodium, 126 mg potassium

Double Chocolate Mint Drops

You can whip up these cookies in no time for a quick chocolate fix.

½ cup butter or margarine, softened
¾ cup sugar
1 egg
½ teaspoon peppermint extract

•••

1 cup all-purpose flour
⅓ cup unsweetened cocoa powder
½ teaspoon baking soda

•••

1 cup semisweet chocolate pieces

In a large mixing bowl, cream butter or margarine and sugar. Beat in the egg and peppermint extract.

In another bowl, combine the flour, cocoa powder, and baking soda. Gradually add the dry ingredients to the butter mixture, mixing just until combined. Stir in the chocolate pieces.

Drop by teaspoons, 2 inches apart, onto ungreased cookie sheets. Bake in a 375° oven for 8 to 10 minutes or until the edges are firm. Cool on a wire rack.

Makes 36 cookies

Per cookie: 78 calories, 1 g protein, 10 g carbohydrate, 4 g total fat (1 g saturated), 6 mg cholesterol, 35 mg sodium, 34 mg potassium

Chocolate-Raisin Thins

Try these crispy "thin" cookies on your afternoon break with a cup of hot tea or coffee.

1 cup butter or margarine, softened
2 cups sugar
2 eggs
1 teaspoon vanilla

•••

2 cups all-purpose flour
⅔ cup unsweetened cocoa powder
1 teaspoon baking soda
¼ teaspoon salt

•••

1 cup raisins

In a large mixing bowl, cream the butter or margarine and sugar. Beat in the eggs and vanilla.

In another bowl, combine the flour, cocoa powder, baking soda, and salt. Gradually add the dry ingredients to the butter mixture, mixing just until combined. Stir in the raisins.

Drop the dough by tablespoons, 2 inches apart, onto a lightly greased cookie sheet. Bake in a 375° oven for 10 to 12 minutes or just until set. Let cookies rest for 1 minute before transferring them from the cookie sheet to cool a wire rack.

Makes 60 cookies

Per cookie: 81 calories, 1 g protein, 13 g carbohydrate, 3 g total fat (2 g saturated), 15 mg cholesterol, 57 mg sodium, 41 mg potassium

Oatmeal-Apricot Cookies

The tartness of dried apricots brightens up this oatmeal cookie.

¼ cup butter or margarine, softened
¼ cup shortening
½ cup sugar
⅓ cup packed brown sugar
1 egg
½ teaspoon vanilla

•••

1¼ cups all-purpose flour
½ teaspoon baking powder
½ teaspoon baking soda
½ teaspoon ground cinnamon
¼ teaspoon salt

•••

1 cup old-fashioned rolled oats
½ cup dried apricots, finely chopped
¼ cup chopped walnuts

In a large mixing bowl, beat together the butter or margarine, shortening, sugar, and brown sugar. Beat in the egg and vanilla.

In another bowl, combine the flour, baking powder, baking soda, cinnamon, and salt. Gradually add the dry ingredients to the sugar mixture and beat just until combined. Stir in the oats, chopped apricots, and chopped walnuts. Cover the dough and chill for 1 hour.

Roll the dough into 1-inch balls, and place them on ungreased cookie sheets. Bake in a 375° oven for 10 to 12 minutes or until the edges are brown. Cool on a wire rack.

Makes 36 cookies

Per cookie: 76 calories, 1 g protein, 10 g carbohydrate, 4 g total fat (1 g saturated), 9 mg cholesterol, 46 mg sodium, 47 mg potassium

Apple-Walnut Turnovers

Wrap a rich cream cheese pastry around apples and walnuts for a tasty dessert or breakfast or brunch treat.

Pastry:

- 1½ cups all-purpose flour
- 2 tablespoons sugar
- ½ cup cold butter
- 1 8-ounce package cold cream cheese

Apple-Walnut Filling:

- 3 to 4 tablespoons sugar
- 1 tablespoon cornstarch
- ½ teaspoon ground cinnamon
- 2 cups tart red apples, finely chopped (2 medium apples)
- 2 tablespoons coarsely chopped walnuts

Pastry: In a large bowl, combine the flour and sugar. With a pastry blender or fork, cut in the butter and cream cheese until the mixture is crumbly. Using your hands, form the mixture into a ball. Wrap dough in plastic wrap and refrigerate for about 1 hour.

Apple-Walnut Filling: In a medium bowl, combine the sugar, cornstarch, and cinnamon. Add the chopped apples and stir to coat with the sugar mixture. Stir in the walnuts.

To assemble, roll half the dough on a lightly floured surface to ⅛-inch thickness. Cut the dough into circles, each 5 to 6 inches in diameter. Repeat with the remaining dough to make a total of 8 to 14 circles. Work quickly before dough becomes too soft.

Place about 2 tablespoons of the filling in the center of each circle. Fold the circles in half and seal by pressing together with your fingers. Press the edges of the dough firmly together with the tines of a fork that have been dipped in flour.

Place the turnovers 2 inches apart on an ungreased cookie sheet. Prick each turnover several times with a fork. Bake in a 350° oven for 20 to 30 minutes or until lightly browned. Serve warm or at room temperature.

Makes 8 to 10 turnovers

Per turnover: 349 calories, 5 g protein, 32 g carbohydrate, 23 g total fat (14 g saturated), 62 mg cholesterol, 202 mg sodium, 104 mg potassium

Cream Cheese Almond Dreams

As a variation, make Orange-Cream Cheese Cookies by omitting the almond extract and almonds and adding 2 teaspoons finely shredded orange peel and ½ teaspoon orange extract.

1 8-ounce package cream cheese,
   softened
½ cup butter or margarine, softened
¾ cup sugar
½ teaspoon almond extract

•••

1½ cups all-purpose flour
2 teaspoons baking powder
⅛ teaspoon salt
½ cup chopped almonds

•••

¼ cup sugar

In a mixing bowl, beat the cream cheese and butter or margarine until fluffy. Add the sugar and almond extract, mixing well.

In another bowl, combine the flour, baking powder, and salt. Gradually add the dry ingredients to the cream cheese mixture, mixing just until combined. Stir in the almonds. Cover the dough and chill for 2 hours.

Roll the cookie dough into 1-inch balls. Roll the balls in sugar, and place them on an ungreased cookie sheet. Press each cookie twice with a fork, making a cross-hatch pattern with the tines. Bake in a 400° oven for 6 to 8 minutes or until the edges just begin to brown.

Makes 60 cookies

Per cookie: 58 calories, 1 g protein, 6 g carbohydrate, 4 g total fat (2 g saturated), 8 mg cholesterol, 27 mg sodium, 18 mg potassium

Ginger-Peach Custard

This peach custard, flavored with almond, vanilla, and gingersnaps, is delicious served warm or at room temperature. Besides being a dessert, it can be part of a leisurely Sunday breakfast or brunch.

2 cups fresh peaches (with or without peel), coarsely chopped, or 2 cups frozen peach slices, thawed and coarsely chopped
¼ cup sugar

Custard:

3 eggs
½ cup half-and-half or light cream
½ cup milk
¼ cup sugar
½ teaspoon almond extract
½ teaspoon vanilla
⅛ teaspoon salt
⅔ cup crushed gingersnap cookies (about 10)

•••

Powdered sugar

Place the chopped peaches in a bowl and toss with sugar. Grease a 10-inch quiche dish; arrange the peaches in a single layer in the dish.

Custard: In a mixing bowl, beat the eggs with a wire whisk. Add the half-and-half or light cream, milk, sugar, almond extract, vanilla, and salt, mixing well. Stir in the crushed gingersnaps, and pour the mixture over the peaches.

Bake in a 350° oven for 30 to 35 minutes or until a knife inserted in the center comes out clean. Dust with powdered sugar. Serve warm. Cover and chill to store.

Serves 6

Per serving: 213 calories, 5 g protein, 35 g carbohydrate, 6 g total fat (2 g saturated), 115 mg cholesterol, 161 mg sodium, 223 mg potassium

Ice Cream with Kiwi, Berries, and Cinnamon

Splurge on your favorite ice cream for this easy dessert fix-up. You may be amazed at the high praise this dessert of exotic flavors will garner.

1 pint vanilla ice cream
1 or 2 kiwifruits, peeled and thinly sliced
4 to 6 strawberries, thinly sliced, or ½ cup blueberries or raspberries
½ cup apricot nectar
Ground cinnamon

Place one large scoop of ice cream in each of 4 dessert glasses. Place a few kiwifruit and strawberry slices around the ice cream. Top each with some of the apricot nectar and a sprinkle of cinnamon.

Serves 4

Per serving: 213 calories, 3 g protein, 25 g carbohydrate, 12 g total fat (7 g saturated), 45 mg cholesterol, 44 mg sodium, 251 mg potassium

Rich and Creamy Hot Fudge Sauce

This chocolate-lover's dream can be served over ice cream, fruit, or dessert. For a special treat, add your favorite liqueur instead of the vanilla.

1 cup unsweetened cocoa powder
¾ cup sugar
½ cup packed brown sugar
⅛ teaspoon salt
½ cup butter or margarine, cut into
    pieces
1 cup whipping cream
1 teaspoon vanilla

In a large saucepan, combine the cocoa powder, sugar, brown sugar, and salt. Add the butter or margarine and cream, mixing well. Place the saucepan over medium heat and bring the mixture to boiling, stirring constantly. Continue cooking, uncovered, for 1 minute, stirring constantly. Remove from the heat and cool for 5 minutes. Stir in the vanilla. Serve warm or cover and store in the refrigerator.

To reheat, place the sauce in a small saucepan and heat over low heat, stirring constantly. Or, place the sauce in a microwave-safe bowl. Microcook, uncovered, on 100% power (high) for about 2 minutes or until heated through, stirring once.

Makes about 2 cups

Per tablespoon: 84 calories, 1 g protein, 9 g carbohydrate, 6 g total fat (4 g saturated), 18 mg cholesterol, 42 mg sodium, 55 mg potassium

Vermont Maple Nut Ice Cream

Serve this rich, maple-flavor ice cream with chocolate cake, or top it with Rich and Creamy Hot Fudge Sauce (page 227).

2 cups half-and-half or light cream
1 cup whole milk
⅓ cup packed brown sugar
⅛ teaspoon salt

•••

5 egg yolks
½ cup pure maple syrup or maple-
** flavor syrup**

•••

½ cup chopped walnuts or pecans

In a saucepan, combine the half-and-half or light cream and milk. Place over medium-high heat and heat just to boiling. Stir in the brown sugar and salt. Remove from heat and let the mixture cool slightly.

In the top of a double boiler, whisk the egg yolks and maple syrup together. Slowly pour a very thin stream of the warm milk mixture into the egg mixture, stirring constantly. (Adding the milk slowly is necessary to prevent the eggs from curdling.) Cook the mixture over low heat, stirring constantly, until the custard thickens and coats the back of a metal spoon (15 to 20 minutes). (The water in the bottom pan of the double boiler should be simmering, not boiling.)

Strain the custard into a large bowl. Let cool to room temperature. Cover and refrigerate overnight before freezing.

Stir the walnuts or pecans into the chilled custard and place in an ice cream freezer. Freeze according to the manufacturer's directions.

Makes 1 quart

Per ½-cup serving: 257 calories, 6 g protein, 24 g carbohydrate, 16 g total fat (6 g saturated), 160 mg cholesterol, 81 mg sodium, 236 mg potassium

Watermelon Ice

Watermelon lovers will fall for this pretty pink ice. Make it on a hot summer day when watermelon season is at its peak. An ice retains its fresh flavor for only a few days, so serve it right away.

5 to 6 cups watermelon chunks
¼ cup sugar
2 teaspoons lemon juice

Remove the seeds from watermelon. Place the watermelon, half at a time, in a food processor container and process until nearly smooth. Pour through a wire-mesh strainer and discard any remaining pulp. Measure 2 cups of watermelon juice, and pour it into a wide, shallow, metal bowl or an 8x8x2-inch baking pan. Add the sugar and lemon juice and stir until the sugar is dissolved.

Put the bowl or pan into the freezer for about 2 hours or until the mixture freezes almost solid. With a large spoon or fork, break the frozen mixture into coarse ice crystals. Return bowl or pan to the freezer for 1 to 2 hours more. Stir again, working quickly to break the mixture into finer ice crystals. Repeat this step at 30 minute intervals 2 more times or until the desired consistency is reached.

Spoon the ice into individual dessert glasses and serve immediately.

Serves 6

Per serving: 75 calories, 1 g protein, 18 g carbohydrate, 1 g total fat (0 g saturated), 0 mg cholesterol, 3 mg sodium, 157 mg potassium

Red Grape Ice

The fresh fruit flavor of red grapes makes this a refreshing, light dessert. Best of all, grapes are available most of the year.

1 **pound seedless red grapes**
¼ **cup sugar**
¼ **cup water**
1 **teaspoon lemon juice**

Wash and stem the grapes. Place in a blender container or food processor bowl and process or blend until smooth. Pour the juice through a wire-mesh strainer and discard the skins. (You should have about 1¼ cups of grape juice.) Pour the juice into a wide, shallow, metal bowl or an 8x8x2-inch baking pan. Add the sugar, water, and lemon juice and stir until the sugar is dissolved. Taste and adjust flavorings, if necessary.

Put the bowl or pan in the freezer for 2 hours or until the mixture freezes solid. With a large spoon or fork, break the frozen mixture into coarse ice crystals. Return bowl or pan to the freezer for 1 to 2 hours more. Stir again, working quickly to break the mixture into finer ice crystals. Repeat this step at 30 minute intervals 2 more times or until the desired consistency is reached.

Spoon into individual dessert glasses and serve immediately.

Serves 4

Per serving: 86 calories, 1 g protein, 22 g carbohydrate, 0 g total fat (0 g saturated), 0 mg cholesterol, 2 mg sodium, 141 mg potassium

Index

Nutrition Analysis

Keep track of your daily nutrition needs by using the information we provide at the end of each recipe. We've analyzed the nutrition content of each recipe serving for you. When a recipe gives an ingredient substitution, we used the first choice in the analysis. If it makes a range of servings (such as 4 to 6), we used the smallest number. Ingredients listed as optional weren't included in the calculations.

Acknowledgments
We would like to express our
gratitude to everyone at Better
Homes and Gardens® Books for
their interest in our cookbook.
Our thanks to the editors and
staff for their professionalism in
handling this project, and the
photographers, food stylists, and
designers whose combined ef-
forts produced such a handsome
publication. Our sincere appre-
ciation to the Test Kitchen for
their adherence to rigorous standards that ensures the highest
quality recipes. And a special
heartfelt thanks to our editor,
Jennifer Darling, for her enthu-
siastic support of our book. It
has been an honor to work with
everyone in the Better Homes
and Gardens® family.

Frank and Jayni
Carey

Metric Conversions

Metric Cooking Hints

By making a few conversions, cooks in Australia, Canada, and the United Kingdom can use the recipes in Better Homes and Gardens® *The Easier You Make It, The Better It Tastes* with confidence. The charts on this page provide a guide for converting measurements from the U.S. customary system, which is used throughout this book, to the imperial and metric systems. There also is a conversion table for oven temperatures to accommodate the differences in oven calibrations.

Volume and Weight: Americans traditionally use cup measures for liquid and solid ingredients. The chart (top right) shows the approximate imperial and metric equivalents. If you are accustomed to weighing solid ingredients, here are some helpful approximate equivalents.
● 1 cup butter, caster sugar, or rice = 8 ounces = about 250 grams
● 1 cup flour = 4 ounces = about 125 grams
● 1 cup icing sugar = 5 ounces = about 150 grams
  Spoon measures are used for smaller amounts of ingredients. Although the size of the tablespoon varies slightly among countries, for practical purposes and for recipes in this book, a straight substitution is all that's necessary.
  Measurements made using cups or spoons should always be level, unless stated otherwise.

Product Differences: Most of the ingredients called for in the recipes in this book are available in English-speaking countries. However, some are known by different names. Here are some common American ingredients and their possible counterparts:
● Sugar is granulated or caster sugar.
● Powdered sugar is icing sugar.
● All-purpose flour is plain household flour or white flour. When self-rising flour is used in place of all-purpose flour in a recipe that calls for leavening, omit the leavening agent (baking soda or baking powder) and salt.
● Light corn syrup is golden syrup.
● Cornstarch is cornflour.
● Baking soda is bicarbonate of soda.
● Vanilla is vanilla essence.

Useful Equivalents

⅛ teaspoon = 0.5ml	⅔ cup = 5 fluid ounces = 150ml
¼ teaspoon = 1ml	¾ cup = 6 fluid ounces = 175ml
½ teaspoon = 2 ml	1 cup = 8 fluid ounces = 250ml
1 teaspoon = 5 ml	2 cups = 1 pint
¼ cup = 2 fluid ounces = 50ml	2 pints = 1 litre
⅓ cup = 3 fluid ounces = 75ml	½ inch =1 centimetre
½ cup = 4 fluid ounces = 125ml	1 inch = 2 centimetres

Baking Pan Sizes

American	Metric
8x1½-inch round baking pan	20x4-centimetre sandwich or cake tin
9x1½-inch round baking pan	23x3.5-centimetre sandwich or cake
11x7x1½-inch baking pan	28x18x4-centimetre baking pan
13x9x2-inch baking pan	32.5x23x5-centimetre baking pan
2-quart rectangular baking dish	30x19x5-centimetre baking pan
15x10x2-inch baking pan	38x25.5x2.5-centimetre baking pan (Swiss roll tin)
9-inch pie plate	22x4- or 23x4-centimetre pie plate
7- or 8-inch springform pan	18- or 20-centimetre springform or loose-bottom cake tin
9x5x3-inch loaf pan narrow loaf pan or paté tin	23x13x6-centimetre or 2-pound
1½-quart casserole	1.5-litre casserole
2-quart casserole	2-litre casserole

Oven Temperature Equivalents

Farenheit Setting	Celsius Setting*	Gas Setting
300°F	150°C	Gas Mark 2
325°F	160°C	Gas Mark 3
350°F	180°C	Gas Mark 4
375°F	190°C	Gas Mark 5
400°F	200°C	Gas Mark 6
425°F	220°C	Gas Mark 7
450°F	230°C	Gas Mark 8
Broil		Grill

Electric and gas ovens may be calibrated using Celsius. However, increase the Celsius setting 10 to 20 degrees when cooking above 160°C with an electric oven. For convection or forced-air ovens (gas or electric), lower the temperature setting 10°C when cooking at all heat levels.